TINY TRAINS

A Guide to Britain's Miniature Railways 2013-2014

EDITOR
John Robinson

Seventh Edition

RAILWAY LOCATOR MAP

The numbers shown on this map relate to the page numbers for each railway.
Pages 5-6 contain an alphabetical listing of the railways featured in this guide.
Please note that the markers on this map show the approximate location only.

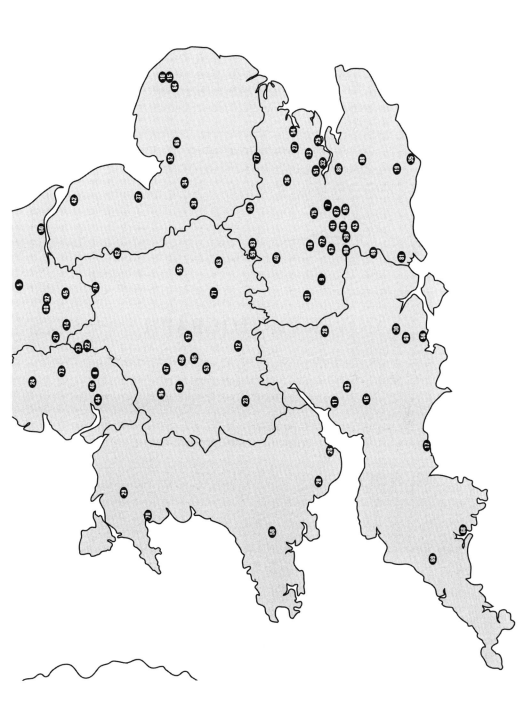

ACKNOWLEDGEMENTS

We were greatly impressed by the friendly and cooperative manner of the staff and helpers of the railways and societies which we selected to appear in this book, and wish to thank them all for the help they have given. In addition we wish to thank Bob Budd (cover design) and Michael Robinson (page layouts) and Jonathan James (photographs) for their help.

Although we believe that the information contained in this guide is accurate at the time of going to press, we, and the Railways and Societies itemised, are unable to accept liability for any loss, damage, distress or injury suffered as a result of any inaccuracies. Furthermore, we and the Societies are unable to guarantee operating and opening times which may always be subject to cancellation without notice. For the purposes of this guide we classify railways with gauges of 7¼ inches or less as 'miniature'.

John Robinson

EDITOR

COVER PHOTOGRAPH

The cover photograph was supplied by Jonathan James and shows the locomotive 'Claudine' at Pecorama's Beer Heights Railway (see page 17) during 2012.

British Library Cataloguing in Publication Data
A catalogue record for this book is available from the British Library

ISBN-13: 978-1-86223-266-2

Copyright © 2013, MARKSMAN PUBLICATIONS. (01472 696226)
72 St. Peter's Avenue, Cleethorpes, N.E. Lincolnshire, DN35 8HU, England

Printed in the UK by Ashford Colour Press Ltd.

CONTENTS

ACTON MINIATURE RAILWAY

Address: London Transport Museum Depot, 118 Gunnersbury Lane, London
Telephone Nº: (020) 7379-6344
Year Formed: 2005
Location of Line: Museum Depot
Length of Line: 100 yards
Unofficial web site: www.actonminiaturerailway.co.uk

Nº of Steam Locos: Visiting locos only
Nº of Other Locos: 1 (plus visiting locos)
Nº of Members: –
Approx Nº of Visitors P.A.: 2,000
Gauge: 7¼ inches

GENERAL INFO

Nearest Mainline Station: South Acton (¾ mile)
Nearest Tube Station: Acton Town (adjacent)
Car Parking: None
Coach Parking: None
Souvenir Shop(s): None
Food & Drinks: None

SPECIAL INFO

The railway is located in the grounds of the London Transport Museum's Depot in Acton and is operated by Friends of the Museum who helped in the line's construction.

OPERATING INFO

Opening Times: During open weekends only, from 11.00am to 5.00pm. Please check the Museum's web site for further details.
Steam Working: Most opening days
Prices: Adults £1.00
Children £1.00
Concessions £1.00

Detailed Directions by Car:
As there is no parking available at the Depot, it is recommended that visitors take the Underground to Acton Town Station which is adjacent.

ALLOSTOCK MINIATURE RAILWAY

Address: All-In-One Garden Centre, London Road, Allostock, Knutsford, Cheshire, WA16 9LU
Telephone Nº: (01565) 722567
Year Formed: 2000
Location: Allostock, near Knutsford

Length of Line: 800 yards
Nº of Steam Locos: None
Nº of Other Locos: Variable
Approx Nº of Visitors P.A.: 12,000
Gauge: 7¼ inches
Web site: www.allinone.co.uk

GENERAL INFORMATION

Nearest Mainline Station: Holmes Chapel (4 miles)
Nearest Bus Station: Holmes Chapel (4 miles)
Car Parking: Spaces for 80 cars on site
Coach Parking: One space available on site
Souvenir Shop(s): Yes
Food & Drinks: Yes

SPECIAL INFORMATION

The Railway runs through the landscaped grounds of the All-In-One Garden Centre in Allostock near Knutsford.

OPERATING INFORMATION

Opening Times: The Railway opens on weekends and Bank Holidays throughout the year. Trains run from 11.00am to 4.30pm (until 4.00pm on Sundays). All train times are weather permitting.
Steam Working: None at present
Prices: £1.00 per ride (Under-3s ride free)

Detailed Directions by Car:
From the North & South: Exit the M6 at Junction 18 and follow the A54 to Holmes Chapel. In Holmes Chapel turn left onto the A50 London Road and follow for 5 miles. All-In-One Garden Centre is on the left hand side.

AMNERFIELD MINIATURE RAILWAY

Address: Amners Farm, Burghfield, Berkshire RG30 3UE	**Nº of Steam Locos:** 3
Telephone Nº: (0118) 988-3063	**Nº of Other Locos:** 5
Year Formed: 1995	**Nº of Members:** 13
Location of Line: Amners Farm	**Approx Nº of Visitors P.A.:** 3,000
Length of Line: ¾ mile	**Gauge:** 5 inches and 7¼ inches
	Web site: www.amnersfarm.co.uk

GENERAL INFORMATION

Nearest Mainline Station: Theale (2 miles)
Nearest Bus Station: Reading
Car Parking: Free parking available on site
Coach Parking: None
Souvenir Shop(s): None
Food & Drinks: Available

OPERATING INFORMATION

Opening Times: 2013 dates: 27th & 28th April; 4th, 5th, 6th & 26th May; 23rd June; 28th July; 25th August and 22nd September.
Trains run from 2.00pm to 5.00pm
Steam Working: Every operating day.
Prices: Adults £1.00

Detailed Directions by Car:
From All Parts: Exit the M4 at Junction 12 and take the A4 towards Reading. After approximately 2 miles turn right at the traffic lights into Burghfield Road. Continue along this road passing over the motorway then take the first turning on the left into Amners Farm Road. After approximately ½ mile turn right into Amners Farm.

ASHMANHAUGH LIGHT RAILWAY

Address: East View Farm, Stone Lane, Ashmanhaugh, Norwich NR12 8YW
Telephone Nº: (01603) 404263
Year Formed: 2002
Location of Line: Near Wroxham Barns
Length of Line: 900 yards

Nº of Steam Locos: 2
Nº of Other Locos: 4
Approx Nº of Visitors P.A.: 2,500
Gauge: 7¼ inches
Web site:
www.ashmanhaughlightrailway.co.uk

GENERAL INFORMATION

Nearest Mainline Station: Wroxham & Hoveton (1½ miles)
Nearest Bus Station: Norwich (10 miles)
Car Parking: Available on site
Coach Parking: None
Souvenir Shop(s): None
Food & Drinks: Light refreshments available

SPECIAL INFORMATION

Close to the Bure Valley Line and the Norwich to Sheringham Line, this is a railway operated by enthusiasts set in the beautiful North Norfolk countryside on a delightful 10 acre landscaped site.

OPERATING INFORMATION

Opening Times: 2013 dates: The first Sunday in the month from 5th May to 6th October inclusive, weather permitting.
Trains run from 2.00pm to 5.00pm.
Steam Working: Most operating days.
Prices: Adults £1.00 (Day Rover ticket £3.00)
Children £1.00 (Day Rover ticket £3.00)
Family Day Rover £10.00 (Unlimited rides)
(2 adults + 2 children)

Detailed Directions by Car:
From All Parts: Ashmanhaugh is situated just off the A1151 Wroxham to Stalham road. The railway is close to the Wroxham Barns Centre and is signposted from the road on open days.

ASHTON COURT ESTATE MINIATURE RAILWAY

Address: Ashton Court Estate, Long Ashton, North Somerset BS8 3PX
Telephone Nº: (0117) 963-9174
Year Formed: Opened 1973
Location of Line: Ashton Court Estate
Length of Line: Two tracks, each approximately a third of a mile in length

Nº of Steam Locos: 3
Nº of Other Locos: 4
Nº of Members: 250
Approx Nº of Visitors P.A.: 30,000
Gauge: 3½ inches, 5 inches & 7¼ inches
Website: www.bristolmodelengineers.co.uk

GENERAL INFORMATION

Nearest Mainline Station: Bristol Temple Meads (Approximately 5 miles)
Nearest Bus Station: Bristol (4 miles)
Car Parking: Parking available on site
Coach Parking: Available by prior arrangement
Souvenir Shop(s): None
Food & Drinks: None

SPECIAL INFORMATION

The Railway is owned and operated by the Bristol Society of Model & Experimental Engineers which was founded in 1909.

OPERATING INFORMATION

Opening Times: Bank Holidays and some Sundays between April and mid-October (22 public passenger carrying days per year). Please contact the railway for a list of dates. On operating days, trains run from 12.00pm to 5.00pm.
Steam Working: All operating days.
Prices: 70p per ride per person. Ticket discounts for multiple rides are available.

Detailed Directions by Car:
Exit the M5 at junction 19 and take the A369 towards Bristol. After approximately 6 miles, just past the B3129 traffic lights is Ashton Court Estate. However, there is no right turn from this direction. Instead, take the side road on the left (North Road), turn right into Bridge Road and continue straight across the A369 at the traffic lights into the Clifton Lodge Entrance. Take the first right then the first right again before the golf kiosk car park.

AVONVALE MODEL ENGINEERING SOCIETY

Address: Hillers, Heath Farm, Alcester Warwickshire B49 5PD
Phone Nº: (01527) 543350
Year Formed: 2001
Location of Line: Hillers, Dunnington
Length of Line: A third of a mile

Nº of Steam Locos: 16
Nº of Other Locos: 12
Nº of Members: Approximately 40
Approx Nº of Visitors P.A.: 3,000
Gauge: 5 inches and 7¼ inches
Web site: www.avonvale.me.uk

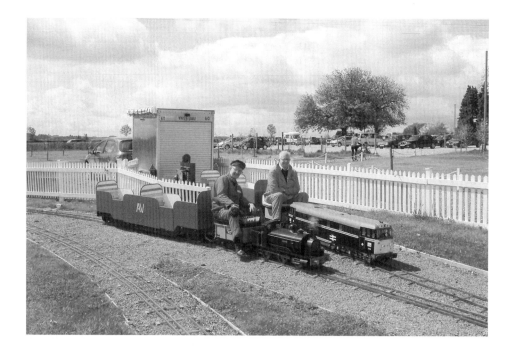

GENERAL INFORMATION

Nearest Mainline Station: Evesham (11 miles)
Nearest Bus Station: Stratford-upon-Avon (13 miles)
Car Parking: Free parking available on site
Coach Parking: None
Souvenir Shop(s): None
Food & Drinks: Available

SPECIAL INFORMATION

The Engines are all privately owned and run as required. The railway is located at Hillers where other attractions include a Café, a Farm Shop and a Display Garden.

OPERATING INFORMATION

Opening Times: 2013 dates: 1st, 20th & 21st April; 4th, 5th, 6th, 25th, 26th & 27th May; 8th, 9th, 22nd and 23rd June; 6th, 7th, 20th & 21st July; 3rd, 4th, 24th, 25th & 26th August; 7th, 8th, 21st & 22nd September; 5th, 6th, 19th, 20th, 30th & 31st October. Trains run from 11.00am to 4.00pm.
Steam Working: Where possible at least two steam locos run on each operating day.
Prices: 80p per ride per person.

Detailed Directions by Car:
From the North: Take the A435 or A46 to Alcester then follow the B4088 to Dunnington. Once in Dunnington, turn right at the crossroad and Hillers is on the right hand side with the railway visible from the road; From the South: Take the Evesham bypass then follow the B4088 to Dunnington.

BARLEYLANDS MINIATURE RAILWAY

Address: Barleylands, Barleylands Road, Billericay, Essex CM11 2UD	**Nº of Steam Locos**: 4
Telephone Nº: (01268) 290229	**Nº of Other Locos**: 1
Year Formed: 1989	**Nº of Members**: None
Location of Line: 3 miles from Billericay	**Approx Nº of Visitors P.A.**: 10,000+
Length of Line: ¼ mile	**Gauge**: 7¼ inches
	Web site: www.barleylands.co.uk

GENERAL INFORMATION

Nearest Mainline Station: Billericay or Basildon
Nearest Bus Station: Billericay or Basildon
Car Parking: Available on site
Coach Parking: Available on site
Souvenir Shop(s): Yes
Food & Drinks: Yes

SPECIAL INFORMATION

The Railway is located in the Barleylands Craft Village and Farm Centre which has a wide range of attractions for all ages. The railway is commercially operated but volunteers help to run and maintain the steam engines.

OPERATING INFORMATION

Opening Times: Daily throughout the year subject to weather conditions. Trains run from 10.00am to 5.00pm (until 4.00pm during the Winter months).
Steam Working: The Railway's steam engines may run at a number of special events. Please contact the railway for further information.
Prices: £1.50 Return (all ages)
Admission to the Park:
    Adults £10.00
    Children £9.00 (Ages 2 to 15 years)
    Concessions £9.00
    Family Ticket £34.00
    (2 adults + 2 children or 1 adult + 3 children)

Detailed Directions by Car:
From M25: Exit at J29 onto A127 (Southend bound) and follow the brown Tourist Information signs for Farm Museum; From the A12: Take the B1007 Billericay junction, towards Stock and follow the brown Tourist Information signs for Farm Museum.

BARNSLEY SOCIETY OF MODEL ENGINEERS

Address: Park Mill Way, Clayton West, near Huddersfield, W. Yorks. HD8 9XJ
Phone Nº: (01226) 763731 (Secretary)
Year Formed: 1955
Location of Line: Kirklees Light Railway, Clayton West
Length of Line: Approximately 650 feet

Nº of Steam Locos: 20
Nº of Other Locos: 4
Nº of Members: 26
Annual Membership Fee: £1.00
Approx Nº of Visitors P.A.: 4,000
Gauges: 3½ inches, 5 inches & 7¼ inches

GENERAL INFORMATION

Nearest Mainline Station: Denby Dale (4 miles)
Nearest Bus Station: Bus stop outside gates. Take the 484 from Wakefield or the 235 and 240 from Huddersfield/Barnsley.
Car Parking: Ample free parking at site
Coach Parking: Ample free parking at site
Souvenir Shop(s): Yes
Food & Drinks: Yes

SPECIAL INFORMATION

The Barnsley S.M.E. track is located at the Kirklees Light Railway.

OPERATING INFORMATION

Opening Times: Trains run from 1.00pm to 5.00pm on Saturdays.
Steam Working: All operating days.
Prices: 50p per ride.

Detailed Directions by Car:
The Railway is located on the A636 Wakefield to Denby Dale road. Turn off the M1 at Junction 39 and follow the A636 signposted for Denby Dale. Continue for approximately 4 miles then the railway is on the left after passing under the railway bridge and is situated at the top of the Industrial Estate, just before the village of Scissett.

Barton House Railway

Address: Hartwell Road, The Avenue, Wroxham   NR12 8TL
Telephone Nº: (01603) 782008
Year Formed: 1963
Location of Line: Wroxham, Norfolk
Length of Line: 167 yards

Nº of Steam Locos: 4
Nº of Other Locos: 4
Approx Nº of Visitors P.A.: 1,250
Gauge: 3½ inches and 7¼ inches
Web site: www.bartonhouserailway.org.uk
Email: enquiries@bartonhouserailway.org.uk

GENERAL INFO

Nearest Mainline Station:
Hoveton and Wroxham (1 mile)
Nearest Bus Station:
Wroxham (1 mile)
Car Parking: Limited parking available on site
Coach Parking: None
Souvenir Shop(s): Yes
Food & Drinks: Available

SPECIAL INFO

The original Honing East signalbox was rebuilt at Wroxham to form the basis for the Barton House Railway which is run entirely by volunteers. On open days, a boat service operates from Wroxham Bridge to take passengers to the railway.

OPERATING INFO

Opening Times: The 3rd Sunday each month from April until October and also on Easter Monday. Trains run from 2.30pm to 5.30pm. Also open on the 4th Saturday in September from 7.00pm to 10.00pm.
Steam Working:
Most operating days.
Prices: Adults £3.00
                 Children £1.50
Note: On open days, access to the railway is also available via an electric launch service running from Wroxham Bridge. Prices of this service are shown above.

Detailed Directions by Car:
From the South and West: Take the A1151 from Norwich to Wroxham then follow the road over the railway bridge. Take the 3rd turning on the right into 'The Avenue', first left into Staitheway Road then right into Hartwell Road. The railway is at the end of the road; From the North: Take the A149 to the A1151 to Wroxham, turn left into 'The Avenue', then as above.

BATH & WEST RAILWAY

Address: The Royal Bath and West Showground, Shepton Mallet, Somerset, BA4 6QN **Phone Nº**: (01749) 840368 (Secretary) **Year Formed**: 2001 **Length of Line**: ½ mile	**Nº of Steam Locos**: 7 **Nº of Other Locos**: 2 **Nº of Members**: Approximately 100 **Annual Membership Fee**: £28.00 **Approx Nº of Visitors P.A.**: 11,000 **Gauge**: 5 inches and 7¼ inches **Web site**: www.essmee.org.uk

GENERAL INFORMATION

Nearest Mainline Station: Castle Cary (4 miles)
Nearest Bus Station: Shepton Mallet
Car Parking: Free parking available on site
Coach Parking: Available
Food & Drinks: Available during shows

SPECIAL INFORMATION

The Bath & West Railway is operated by members of the East Somerset Society of Model and Experimental Engineers.

OPERATING INFORMATION

Opening Times: The railway is situated on The Royal Bath and West Showground. Our operating days, as well as our ability to entertain visitors with their locos, are therefore governed by which particular shows are using the showground. The railway operates on the four days of the Royal Bath & West Show from 29th May to 1st June 2013. Agreements between the Society and other shows may mean that the railway also operates on other dates during July and August 2013. Please contact the Society for further information and please check dates before visiting. The Society's open weekend is planned for 28th & 29th September 2013 when members of the public and other Engineering Societies are invited to visit with their locos.
Steam Working: All operating days.
Prices: £1.50 per ride   Day tickets are £10.00

Detailed Directions by Car:
From All Parts: The Royal Bath and West Showground is situated approximately 2 miles south of Shepton Mallet just off the A371 road to Castle Cary.

BEER HEIGHTS LIGHT RAILWAY

Address: Pecorama, Beer, East Devon, EX12 3NA	**Nº of Steam Locos**: 7 at present
Telephone Nº: (01297) 21542	**Nº of Other Locos**: 2
Year Formed: 1975	**Approx Nº of Visitors P.A.**: 60,000
Location of Line: Beer, East Devon	**Gauge**: 7¼ inches
Length of Line: 1 mile	**Web site**: www.pecorama.info
	E-mail: pecorama@pecobeer.co.uk

GENERAL INFORMATION

Nearest Mainline Station: Axminster
Nearest Bus Stop: Beer
Car Parking: Available on site
Coach Parking: Available on site
Souvenir Shop(s): Yes
Food & Drinks: Licensed restaurant on site

SPECIAL INFORMATION

In addition to the Railway, Pecorama features a Model Railway Exhibition, childrens activity areas and extensive gardens.

OPERATING INFORMATION

Opening Times: 2013 dates: Open weekdays from 25th March to 1st November and also on Saturday and Sunday from 25th May to 8th September.
Steam Working: On every operating day.
Prices: Adult £8.00
              Child £6.50 (Under-4s free of charge)
              Senior Citizens £7.50 (Over-80s free)
The prices above include one ride on the railway and entry to the Gardens and other attractions at Pecorama.

Detailed Directions by Car:
From All Parts: Take the A3052 to Beer, turn onto the B3174 and follow the Brown Tourist signs for Pecorama.

BEKONSCOT LIGHT RAILWAY

Address: Bekonscot Model Village & Railway, Warwick Road, Beaconsfield, Bucks   HP9 2PL
Telephone Nº: (01494) 672919
Year Formed: 2001
Location of Line: Beaconsfield, Bucks.
Length of Line: 400 yards

Nº of Steam Locos: None at present
Nº of Other Locos: 3
Nº of Members: –
Approx Nº of Visitors P.A.: 180,000
Gauge: 7¼ inches
Web site: www.bekonscot.com

GENERAL INFORMATION

Nearest Mainline Station:
Beaconsfield (5 minutes walk)
Nearest Bus Station: High Wycombe
Car Parking: Limited spaces adjacent to the site
Coach Parking: Limited spaces adjacent to the site
Souvenir Shop(s): Yes
Food & Drinks: Available

SPECIAL INFORMATION

The Railway is situated in Bekonscot Model Village, a 1½ acre miniature landscape of fields, farms, castles, churches, woods and lakes which also contains a model railway.

OPERATING INFORMATION

Opening Times: 2013 dates: Daily from 16th February to 3rd November. Open 10.00am to 5.00pm (trains run from 11.00am to 4.30pm).
Steam Working: None at present
Prices: Adult £9.50
Child £5.50 (Ages 2–15 years)
Family Ticket £26.00
Senior Citizens £7.00 (£6.00 on weekdays)
Concessions £7.00 (£6.00 on weekdays)
Note: Prices shown above are for entrance into Bekonscot Model Village which is required to visit the railway. Rides are an additional £1.00 per person.

Detailed Directions by Car:
From All Parts: Exit the M40 at Junction 2 taking the A355 then follow the signs for the "Model Village".

BENTLEY MINIATURE RAILWAY

Address: Bentley Country Park,
Halland   BN8 5AF
Telephone Nº: 0845 862-2583
Year Formed: 1985
Location of Line: 5 miles North of Lewes
Length of Line: 1 mile

Nº of Steam Locos: Members locos only
Nº of Other Locos: Members locos only
Approx Nº of Visitors P.A.: 50,000 (to the Museum)
Gauge: 5 inches and 7¼ inches
Web site: www.bentleyrailway.co.uk

GENERAL INFORMATION

Nearest Mainline Station: Uckfield (4 miles)
Nearest Bus Station: Uckfield (4 miles)
Car Parking: Free parking available on site
Coach Parking: Free parking available on site
Souvenir Shop(s): Yes
Food & Drinks: Available

SPECIAL INFORMATION

The railway is owned and operated by members of the Uckfield Model Railway Club and is located in the grounds of the Bentley Wildfowl & Motor Museum (www.bentley.org.uk) which houses a wide range of other attractions.

OPERATING INFORMATION

Opening Times: Sundays throughout the year. Weekends from Easter to the end of October and daily during most East Sussex School Holidays throughout the year. Trains run from 11.30am to 4.00pm (5.00pm from Easter to end of October).
Steam Working: Most Sundays.
Prices: Adults £8.00 (Museum Entry only)
   Children £6.00 (Museum Entry only)
   Concessions £7.00 (Museum Entry only)
   Family £26.00 (Museum Entry only)
Note: Train rides are an additional £1.00 per person.

E-mail: enquiries@uckfieldmrc.co.uk

Detailed Directions by Car:
From All Parts: Bentley Wildfowl & Motor Museum is located just outside of the village of Shortgate by the B2192 road between Halland (which located by at the junction of the B2192 and A22) and Lewes (A26/A27). The Museum is well-signposted locally from the A22 (Uckfield to Eastbourne), A26 (Uckfield to Lewes) and B2192.

BRIDGEND & DISTRICT M.E.S.

Address: Fountain Road, Tondu, Bridgend   CF32 0EH
Telephone Nº: (01656) 740480
Year Formed: 1984
Location of Line: Tondu, near Bridgend
Length of Line: 1,600 feet

Nº of Steam Locos: 6
Nº of Other Locos: 6
Nº of Members: Approximately 45
Approx Nº of Visitors P.A.: 800
Gauge: 3½ inches, 5 inches & 7¼ inches
Website: www.bridgendminiaturerailway.com

GENERAL INFORMATION

Nearest Mainline Station: Tondu (1 mile)
Nearest Bus Station: Bridgend (2 miles)
Car Parking: Available on site
Coach Parking: Available on site
Food & Drinks: Available

SPECIAL INFORMATION

A 4-inch scale traction engine is available to give rides on most of the Society's open days.

OPERATING INFORMATION

Opening Times: The first Saturday of each month from April to October inclusive. Also on Bank Holiday Mondays. Please contact the railway for further details. Trains run from noon until 4.00pm.
Steam Working: All open days where possible.
Prices: £1.00 per person per ride.
Note: The line is available for birthday party bookings. Please contact the Society for details.

Detailed Directions by Car:
Exit the M4 at Junction 36 and follow the A4063 Northwards. At the first roundabout take the 2nd exit onto the B4281 Park Road. Continue into Fountain Road and turn right (still on Fountain Road). The MES club area is located opposite the entrance to Parc Slip Nature Reserve.

BRIGHOUSE & HALIFAX MODEL ENGINEERS

Address: Ravensprings Park, Cawcliffe Road, Brighouse   HD6 2HP
Telephone N°: (01484) 717140
Year Formed: 1932
Location of Line: Ravensprings Park
Length of Line: 650 feet (5 inch gauge) and 1,200 feet (7¼ inch gauge)

N° of Steam Locos: 50-60
N° of Other Locos: 2 (traction engines)
N° of Members: Approximately 75
Approx N° of Visitors P.A.: 4,500
Gauge: 2½ inches, 3½ inches, 5 inches and 7¼ inches
Web site: www.bhme.co.uk

GENERAL INFORMATION

Nearest Mainline Station: Brighouse (1½ miles)
Nearest Bus Station: Brighouse (1 mile)
Car Parking: Available on site
Coach Parking: Available by prior arrangement
Food & Drinks: Available on open days

OPERATING INFORMATION

Opening Times: Open to the public on the second Sunday of each month from April to October inclusive. Trains run from 1.30pm to 5.00pm.
Steam Working: All operating days.
Prices: Adults £3.00 (unlimited rides)
Children £2.00 (unlimited rides)

Detailed Directions by Car:
Ravensprings Park lies in the Northern part of Brighouse. From the South: Take the A641 Bradford Road northwards and turn left just after the Thaal Indian Restaurant into Cross Street for Smith Carr Lane. Turn right into Bracken Road then left into Cawcliffe Road for the Park; From the North: Travel into Brighouse on the A641 and turn right just before the Thaal Indian Restaurant into Cross Street. Then as above.

BROOKSIDE MINIATURE RAILWAY

Address: London Road North (A523), Poynton, Cheshire SK12 1BY
Telephone Nº: (01625) 872919
Year Formed: 1989
Location: Brookside Garden Centre
Length of Line: Approximately ½ mile

Nº of Steam Locos: 5
Nº of Other Locos: 3
Approx Nº of Visitors P.A.: 95,000
Gauge: 7¼ inches
Web site:
www.brookside-miniature-railway.co.uk

GENERAL INFORMATION

Nearest Mainline Station: Poynton and Hazel Grove (both 1 mile)
Nearest Bus Station: Stockport (5 miles).
Car Parking: 400 spaces available on site
Coach Parking: 2 spaces available
Souvenir Shop(s): Yes
Food & Drinks: Yes

SPECIAL INFORMATION

The Railway runs through the grounds of the Brookside Garden Centre. There is also an extensive collection of Railwayana on display.

OPERATING INFORMATION

Opening Times: The Railway is open on weekends and Bank Holidays plus Wednesdays from April to September. Open every day in July and August as well as during School holidays. Trains usually run from 10.45am to 4.30pm but only until 4.00pm from November to February.
Steam Working: Weekends and Bank Holidays only
Prices: Adult £1.50 per ride (10 ride tickets £11.00)
         Child £1.50 per ride (10 ride tickets £11.00)
Note: Under-2s ride for free

Detailed Directions by Car:
From the North: Exit the M60 at Junction 1 in Stockport and take the A6 (signposted Buxton). Upon reaching Hazel Grove, take the A523 to Poynton. Follow the brown tourist signs for the Railway; From the West: Exit the M56 at Junction 6 signposted Wilmslow and continue to Poynton. Follow the brown signs for the Railway; From the South: Exit the M6 at Junction 18 for Holmes Chapel. Follow the signs to Wilmslow, then as from the West; From the East: Follow the A6 to Hazel Grove, then as from the North.

BROOMY HILL RAILWAY

Address: Broomy Hill, Hereford **Telephone Nº:** (01989) 762119 **Year Formed:** 1962 **Location of Line:** Adjacent to the Waterworks Museum, Hereford **Length of Line:** 1 kilometre	**Nº of Steam Locos:** 4+ **Nº of Other Locos:** 1+ **Nº of Members:** Approximately 80 **Approx Nº of Visitors P.A.:** Not known **Gauge:** 7¼ inches, 5 inches, 3½ inches **Web site:** www.hsme.co.uk

GENERAL INFORMATION

Nearest Mainline Station: Hereford (1½ miles)
Nearest Bus Station: Hereford (1½ miles)
Car Parking: Free parking available on site
Coach Parking: Available by prior arrangement
Souvenir Shop(s): Yes
Food & Drinks: Available

SPECIAL INFORMATION

The Broomy Hill Railway is operated by the
Hereford Society of Model Engineers and has two
separate tracks which run along the bank of the
River Wye. Members run their own locomotives so
the number and variety in operation may vary from
day to day. Entry to the site is free of charge and
picnic areas are available.

OPERATING INFORMATION

Opening Times: 2013 dates: 1st, 14th & 28th April;
12th & 26th May; 9th June; 14th & 28th July;
11th August; 8th & 29th September; 13th & 27th
October; 2nd November.
Trains run from 12.00pm to 4.30pm.
Steam Working: All operating days.
Prices: Adults £1.50 per ride
Children £1.50 per ride
Note: Four rides can be bought for £5.00 and
children's parties can be arranged.

Detailed Directions by Car:
From the centre of Hereford, take the A49 Ross-on-Wye Road, turning right into Barton Road. After approximately
400 metres, turn left into Broomy Hill Road, proceed for around 600 metres before turning left following signs
for the Waterworks Museum. The railway is on the right just after the museum which is signposted with Brown
Tourist Information Signs.

BURNLEY & PENDLE MINIATURE RAILWAY

Contact Telephone Nº: 07957 714148
Year Formed: 1992
Location: Thompson Park, Ormerod Road, Burnley BB11 2AA
Length of Line: 1 mile
Gauge: 7¼ inches
Web site: www.bpmrs.org.uk

Nº of Steam Locos: 2 (Member's locos)
Nº of Other Locos: 6
Nº of Members: 33
Annual Membership Fee: £10.00 Adults, £6.00 Concessions, Students & Children
Approx Nº of Visitors P.A.: 7,000

GENERAL INFORMATION

Nearest Mainline Station: Burnley Central (1 mile)
Nearest Bus Station: Burnley (1 mile)
Car Parking: Available adjacent to Thompson Park
Coach Parking: Not available
Food & Drinks: Available from a kiosk in the Park

SPECIAL INFORMATION

A wheelchair accessible coach has been acquired via a lottery grant.

OPERATING INFORMATION

Opening Times: Sundays and Bank Holiday Mondays from Easter until the end of September. Also on Wednesdays during the Summer School holidays. Trains run between 12.00pm and 4.00pm.
Steam Working: Most operating days.
Prices: £1.00 per person per ride
Note: Dogs are not allowed in Thompson Park!

Detailed Directions by Car:
The Railway runs through Thompson Park in Burnley. The main entrance to this is in Ormerod Road which is just a short distance from the town centre and also near to Turf Moor, the home of Burnley FC.

CANVEY MINIATURE RAILWAY

Address: Waterside Farm Sports Centre, Somnes Avenue, Canvey Island, Essex, SS8 9RA
Telephone Nº: (01268) 681679
Year Formed: 1977
Location of Line: Canvey Island
Length of Line: Two lines, one of 1,440 feet and one of 4,400 feet (7¼ inch line)

Nº of Steam Locos: Variable
Nº of Other Locos: Variable
Nº of Members: Approximately 100
Approx Nº of Visitors P.A.: 6,000
Gauge: 3½ inches, 5 inches & 7¼ inches
Web site: www.cramec.org

GENERAL INFORMATION

Nearest Mainline Station: Benfleet (1 mile)
Nearest Bus Station: Bus stop just outside
Car Parking: Available on site
Coach Parking: Available on site
Food & Drinks: None

SPECIAL INFORMATION

The railway is operated by members of the Canvey Railway and Model Engineering Club.

OPERATING INFORMATION

Opening Times: 2013 dates: Every Sunday from the 31st March until 13th October. Also open for Santa Specials on dates during December. Please contact the railway for further information. Trains run from 10.30am to 4.00pm.
Steam Working: When available on operating days.
Prices: £1.00 per ride.
Also £5.00 for 6 rides or £9.00 for 12 rides.

Detailed Directions by Car:
All road routes to Canvey Island meet at the Waterside Farm roundabout. The railway lines are located in the grounds of the Sports Complex/Leisure Centre. Turn right at the traffic lights into the centre and the car park is on the left with the railway on the right.

CARDIFF MODEL ENGINEERING SOCIETY

Address: Heath Park, King George V
Drive, Cardiff CF14 4EN
Telephone Nº: (029) 2075-5731
Year Formed: 1948
Location of Line: Heath Park, Cardiff
Length of Line: 2 tracks of 1,000 feet
each plus a tram track of 700 feet

Nº of Steam Locos: 8
Nº of Other Locos: 4
Nº of Members: Approximately 150
Approx Nº of Visitors P.A.: 7,000
Gauge: 3½ inches, 5 inches & 7¼ inches
Web site: www.cardiffmes.com

GENERAL INFORMATION

Nearest Mainline Station: Heath Low Level (½ mile)
Nearest Bus Station: Cardiff
Car Parking: Available on site and also nearby
Coach Parking: None
Food & Drinks: Available

SPECIAL INFORMATION

The Cardiff Model Engineering society moved to
Heath Park in 1987. The site, which includes two
railway tracks and a unique electric tramway, two
model railways, and extensive refreshment facilities,
has been developed by the members for the benefit
of visitors.

OPERATING INFORMATION

Opening Times: 2013 public dates: 17th & 31st
March; 1st & 28th April; 26th & 27th May;
30th June; 21st July; 26th August; 22nd September;
20th October. Also a ticket-only Santa Special
service on 1st December (Note: These Santa Special
tickets are only on sale on 22nd September).
Trains run from 1.00pm to 5.00pm.
Steam Working: All operating days.
Prices: £1.50 entry per person then £1.50 per ride.
Children aged 3 and under are admitted and ride
free of charge.
Please note that prices may be subject to change.

Detailed Directions by Car:
Exit the M4 at Junction 32 and travel towards Cardiff. Turn left at the 3rd set of traffic lights (by the Tesco garage)
and continue through 3 sets of traffic lights to the T-junction lights. Turn left here then immediately right then
take the 1st left onto King George V Drive. Turn left at the roundabout and take the lane 400 yards on the right.

Chelmsford Society Model Engineers

Address: Meteor Way (off Waterhouse Lane), Chelmsford, Essex CM1 2RL
Telephone Nº: None
Year Formed: 1935
Location of Line: Chelmsford
Length of Line: Two tracks, each approximately 1,000 feet long

Nº of Steam Locos: 40+ (owned by
Nº of Other Locos: 10+   members)
Nº of Members: Approximately 75
Approx Nº of Visitors P.A.: 1,500
Gauge: 3½ inches, 5 inches & 7¼ inches
Web site:
www.chelmsford-miniature-railway.org.uk

GENERAL INFORMATION

Nearest Mainline Station: Chelmsford (½ mile)
Nearest Bus Station: Chelmsford (½ mile)
Car Parking: Available adjacent to the railway (currently free of charge at weekends)
Food & Drinks: Light refreshments available

SPECIAL INFORMATION

The Chelmsford Society of Model Engineers promotes the safe construction and operation of passenger-carrying steam, electric and diesel hauled trains, traction engines and other scale models.

OPERATING INFORMATION

Opening Times: 2013 dates: Every Sunday from 28th April to 6th October inclusive. Santa Specials also run on 1st December (pre-booking is required for this service). Trains usually run from 2.00pm to 4.30pm but a Special Open Day is to be held on 8th September when the site is open from 10.00am. Please check the Society's web site for further details.
Steam Working: Most operating days.
Prices: 50p per person per ride. 12 rides are available for the price of £5.00

Detailed Directions by Car:
From London: Follow the A12 then take the A1016 towards Chelmsford town centre. Continue past the A414 junctions into Westway then into Waterhouse Lane. Meteor Way is on the right after the fourth set of traffic lights, just before the river. Park and then proceed past the five bar gate to the club entrance on the right; From Southend: Follow the A130 to the A12 junction then cross onto the A1114. After 1¼ miles join the A414 towards Chelmsford. Follow the A414 around Chelmsford to the junction with the A1016 at Widford. Take the 2nd exit into Westway then as from London; From Colchester: Follow the A12 and exit at the A414 junction towards Chelmsford. Follow the A414 to the A1016, then as from Southend.

COATE WATER PARK MINIATURE RAILWAY

Address: Coate Water Country Park, Swindon, Wiltshire SN3 6AA
Telephone Nº: (01666) 577596 (Secretary)
Year Formed: 1964
Location of Line: Coate Water Country Park, Swindon
Length of Line: ½ mile

Nº of Steam/Other Locos: A number of different locos are supplied for use by members of the Society
Nº of Members: Approximately 80
Approx Nº of Visitors P.A.: 26,000
Gauge: 5 inches and 7¼ inches
Web site: www.nwmes.info

GENERAL INFORMATION

Nearest Mainline Station: Swindon (2 miles)
Nearest Bus Station: Swindon (2 miles)
Car Parking: Available in the Park
Coach Parking: None
Food & Drinks: Available in the Park

SPECIAL INFORMATION

The Coate Water Park Miniature Railway is operated by volunteers from the North Wiltshire Model Engineering Society.

OPERATING INFORMATION

Opening Times: Sundays and most Saturdays, weather permitting. Open from 11.00am with trains running until approximately 5.00pm.
Please contact the railway for further information.
Steam Working: Depends which locos have been provided for use on the day by the individual members.
Prices: £1.00 per person per ride.

Detailed Directions by Car:
From Junction 15 of the M4, take the A419 North. Take the first exit left onto the A4259 towards Swindon and follow the dual-carriageway past the Great Western Hospital then turn left at the roundabout for Coate Water Park and follow the road to the main car park. From the car park walk round to the left for the railway.

CONWY VALLEY RAILWAY MUSEUM

Address: Old Goods Yard, Betws-y-Coed, Conwy, North Wales LL24 0AL	**Nº of Steam Locos**: 4
Telephone Nº: (01690) 710568	**Nº of Other Locos**: 2
Year Formed: 1983	**Approx Nº of Visitors P.A.**: 50,000
Location of Line: Betws-y-Coed	**Gauge**: 7¼ inches and 15 inches
Length of Line: One and an eighth miles	**Web site**: www.conwyrailwaymuseum.co.uk

GENERAL INFORMATION

Nearest Mainline Station: Betws-y-Coed (20 yards)
Nearest Bus Station: 40 yards
Car Parking: Car park at site
Coach Parking: Car park at site
Souvenir Shop(s): Yes
Food & Drinks: Yes – Buffet Coach Cafe

SPECIAL INFORMATION

The Museum houses the unique 3D dioramas by the late Jack Nelson. Also the ¼ size steam loco 'Britannia'. The railway has rebuilt two Denver and Rio Grande C16 locomotives for use on the line. It also operates an Isle of Man loco – "Douglas".

OPERATING INFORMATION

Opening Times: Daily from 10.00am to 5.00pm.
Trains Working: Daily from 10.15am
Prices: Adult – £1.50 museum entry;
Train rides £1.50; Tram rides £1.00
Child/Senior Citizen – 80p museum entry;
Train rides £1.50; Tram rides £1.00
Family tickets – £4.00
Note: Tram rides are available a 15 inch gauge single-deck tram using a specially-built ½ mile track running alongside the mainline.
'Toby', a self-drive electric tram for children runs on a 7¼ inch gauge track by the Coach Cafe.

Detailed Directions by Car:
From Midlands & South: Take M54/M6 onto the A5 and into Betws-y-Coed; From Other Parts: Take the A55 coast road then the A470 to Betws-y-Coed. The museum is located by the Mainline Station directly off the A5.

Cuckoo Hill Railway

Address: Avon Valley Nurseries,
South Gorley   SP6 2PP
Telephone Nº: (01425) 652003
Year Formed: 1991
Location: Near Ringwood, Hampshire
Length of Line: 900 yards

Nº of Steam Locos: 1
Nº of Other Locos: None
Approx Nº of Visitors P.A.: 7,000
Gauge: 7¼ inches
Web site: www.avonvalleynurseries.co.uk

GENERAL INFORMATION

Nearest Mainline Station: Salisbury (12 miles)
Nearest Bus Station: Salisbury (12 miles)
Car Parking: Available on site
Coach Parking: Available in the Village
Souvenir Shop(s): None
Food & Drinks: Available

SPECIAL INFORMATION

Cuckoo Hill Railway is one of the earliest railways to operate at a garden centre in the UK.

OPERATING INFORMATION

Opening Times: Weekends and Bank Holiday Mondays from Easter to the end of October. Also open on Thursdays and Fridays during the School Holidays. Trains run from 11.00am to 5.00pm.
Steam Working: Every operating day.
Prices: £1.50 per ride

Detailed Directions by Car:
From All Parts: South Gorley is situated on the A338 between Ringwood and Fordingbridge and the Nurseries are just to the east of the road.

CUTTESLOWE PARK MINIATURE RAILWAY

Address: Cutteslowe Park, Harbord Road, Oxford OX2 8ES	**Nº of Steam Locos:** 40
Phone Nº: (01367) 700550 (Secretary)	**Nº of Other Locos:** 10
Year Formed: 1955	**Nº of Members:** Approximately 110
Location: Cutteslowe Park, Oxford	**Approx Nº of Visitors P.A.:** 10,000
Length of Line: Two lines – 390 yard raised line and 250 yard ground level line	**Gauge:** 3½ inches, 5 inches & 7¼ inches
	Web site: www.cosme.org.uk

GENERAL INFORMATION

Nearest Mainline Station: Oxford (3¼ miles)
Nearest Bus Station: Oxford (3 miles)
Car Parking: Available on site
Coach Parking: Available by prior arrangement
Food & Drinks: Refreshments are available in Cutteslowe Park

SPECIAL INFORMATION

The Cutteslowe Park Miniature Railway is operated by the City of Oxford Society of Model Engineers.

OPERATING INFORMATION

Opening Times: The railway opens on the 1st, 3rd and 5th Sundays of each month as well as Bank Holidays from Easter to the end of October. Trains run from 1.30pm to 5.00pm. Trains also run on Wednesdays in the School Summer Holidays in July and August – 1.00pm to 4.30pm.
Steam Working: Up to 5 steam locomotives run on every operating day.
Prices: Adults £1.00   Children £1.00
10 rides are available for £8.00

Detailed Directions by Car:
From outside of Oxford join the ringroad and head to the North of the city. At the roundabout at the junction of the A40 ringroad and the A4165 Banbury Road, head North signposted for Kidlington. Take the third turn on the right into Harbord Road which leads directly into the Park. Follow the signs from the car park for the Railway.

DOCKLAND & EAST LONDON M.E.S.

Address: Belhus Woods Country Park, Romford Road, Aveley, Essex
Phone N°: (01708) 222658 (Secretary)
Year Formed: 1985
Location: Belhus Woods Country park
Length of Line: 500 feet

N° of Steam Locos: 1
N° of Other Locos: 3
N° of Members: 22
Approx N° of Visitors P.A.: 400
Gauge: 5 inches and 7¼ inches

GENERAL INFORMATION

Nearest Mainline Station: Upminster (4 miles)
Nearest Bus Station: Grays (5 miles)
Car Parking: Pay & Display parking available on site
Coach Parking: Available by prior arrangement
Souvenir Shop(s): Yes – Country Park shop
Food & Drinks: Light refreshments available

SPECIAL INFORMATION

The Railway is located in Belhus Woods which is a beautiful Country Park which has picnic areas adjacent to the track and woodland walks through areas full of waterfowl.

OPERATING INFORMATION

Opening Times: During the first Sunday and on Bank Holiday Mondays of every month from April to October inclusive.
Trains run from 1.00pm to 4.30pm.
Steam Working: Weather permitting, both Steam-hauled and Electric services should run on every operating day.
Prices: 50p per person per ride.

Detailed Directions by Car:
Exit the M25 at Junction 29 and follow the A127 towards Romford. After 1 mile turn off at the Hall Lane exit by the flyover and head South towards Upminster. Continue down Hall Lane following through into Station Road then Corbets Tey Road. Upon reaching the T-junction turn right into Harwood Hall Lane then left at the mini-roundabout into Aveley Road. Belhus Woods Country Park is on the left after about 1¼ miles.

DRAGON MINIATURE RAILWAY

Address: Marple Garden Centre, Dooley Lane, Marple, Stockport SK6 7HE
Telephone Nº: 07748 581160
Year Formed: 1999
Location of Line: Marple Garden Centre
Length of Line: ½ mile

Nº of Steam Locos: 5
Nº of Other Locos: 5
Approx Nº of Visitors P.A.: 30,000
Gauge: 7¼ inches
Web site: www.freewebs.com/dragonrailway/

GENERAL INFORMATION

Nearest Mainline Station: Romley (1 mile)
Nearest Bus Station: Stockport (2½ miles)
Car Parking: Available on site
Coach Parking: Available
Souvenir Shop(s): Yes
Food & Drinks: Available

SPECIAL INFORMATION

Dragon Miniature Railway is one of the few Garden Centre-based railways which operates steam on most open days.

OPERATING INFORMATION

Opening Times: Weekends and Bank Holidays throughout the year. Trains run from 11.00am to 4.30pm.
Steam Working: Most operating days.
Prices: £1.00 per ride (Under-2s free of charge)
Ten-ride tickets are available for £8.00

Detailed Directions by Car:
From All Parts: Exit the M60 at Junction 25, pass through Bredbury and follow signs for Marple along the A627. Cross over the River Goyt and Marple Garden Centre is on the left.

DUNHAM'S WOOD LIGHT RAILWAY

Address: Dunham's Wood, Rodham Road, March   PE15 0DN
Phone Nº: (01760) 338052 (Chairman)
Year Formed: 1989
Location of Line: Just off the B1099 in March, Cambridgeshire
Length of Line: Approximately ½ mile

Nº of Steam Locos: None
Nº of Other Locos: 8
Nº of Members: Approximately 20
Approx Nº of Visitors P.A.: 1,200
Gauge: 7¼ inches
Website: dunhamswoodlightrailway.webs.com

GENERAL INFORMATION

Nearest Mainline Station: March (3 miles)
Nearest Bus Station: March (2 miles)
Car Parking: Available on site
Coach Parking: Available on site
Food & Drinks: Available on open days

SPECIAL INFORMATION

The railway runs through a woodland containing various art structures, a maze and a tearoom.

OPERATING INFORMATION

Opening Times: 2013 dates: 1st April; 5th, 6th, 26th & 27th May; 28th July; 25th & 26th August; 15th September. A number of other dates are provisionally planned. Please contact the railway for further information. Trains run from 2.00pm to 5.00pm on all operating days.
Steam Working: Only when steam locos visit.
Prices: Adults £1.00
             Children 50p (Under-5s ride free)
Note: An extra fee of £2.00 is also charged for entrance to the Wood.

Detailed Directions by Car:
From the A141 North or South, follow directions to March town centre. From here follow the B1099 signposted for Christchurch. After 1 mile cross the railway line then take the next turning on the left into Binnimoor Road. After 1 mile turn right into Rodham Road and the wood is on the left after 200 metres with the Car Park opposite.

EASTBOURNE MINIATURE STEAM RAILWAY

Address: Lottbridge Drove, Eastbourne, East Sussex   BN23 6QJ
Telephone Nº: (01323) 520229
Year Formed: 1992
Location of Line: Eastbourne
Length of Line: 1 mile

Nº of Steam Locos: 8
Nº of Other Locos: 3
Approx Nº of Visitors P.A.: Not known
Gauge: 7¼ inches
Web site: www.emsr.co.uk

GENERAL INFORMATION

Nearest Mainline Station: Eastbourne (2 miles)
Nearest Bus Station: Eastbourne (2 miles)
Car Parking: Free parking on site
Coach Parking: Free parking on site
Souvenir Shop(s): Yes
Food & Drinks: Yes

SPECIAL INFORMATION

The Railway site also has many other attractions including model railways, an adventure playground, nature walk, picnic area and a Cafe.

OPERATING INFORMATION

Opening Times: 2013 dates: Open daily from 23rd March until 29th September. Also special events on Easter Sunday and on weekends during October. Trains run from 10.00am to 5.00pm.
Steam Working: Weekends, Bank Holidays and during School Holidays. Diesel at other times.
Prices: Adult £4.85
        Child £4.35 (2 years and under free)
        Family Tickets £17.50
                    (2 adults + 2 children)

Detailed Directions by Car:
From All Parts: Take the A22 new road to Eastbourne then follow the Brown tourist signs for the 'Mini Railway'.

East Herts Miniature Railway

Address: Van Hage Garden Centre, Great Amwell, near Ware SG12 9RP
Telephone Nº: (020) 8292-2997
Year Formed: 1978
Location: Van Hage Garden Centre
Length of Line: 500 metres

Nº of Steam Locos: 3
Nº of Other Locos: 2
Nº of Members: Approximately 40
Annual Membership Fee: £16.00
Approx Nº of Visitors P.A.: 40,000
Gauge: 7¼ inches
Web site: www.ehmr.org.uk

GENERAL INFORMATION

Nearest Mainline Station: Ware (1½ miles)
Nearest Bus Station: Bus stop outside the Centre
Car Parking: Available on site
Coach Parking: Available
Food & Drinks: Available in the Garden Centre

SPECIAL INFORMATION

The Railway operates a line at the Van Hage Garden Centre in Great Amwell. The railway is run by volunteers and any profits are donated to the local special needs school and other local charities.

OPERATING INFORMATION

Opening Times: Weekends and Bank Holidays throughout the year. Also open Tuesdays and Thursdays during the school holidays. Usually open from 11.00am to 5.00pm but from 10.30am to 4.30pm on Sundays.
Steam Working: Most operating days.
Prices: 90p per person per ride. Under-2s travel free of charge.

Detailed Directions by Car:
From the South: Take the A10 towards Cambridge and exit at the first Ware junction signposted for A414. Take the 2nd exit at the roundabout onto the A1170 towards Ware and Van Hage Garden Centre is on the left after 600 metres; From the East: Take the A414 from Harlow and turn off onto the A1170 for Ware. Then as above.

EVERGREENS MINIATURE RAILWAY

Address: Main Road, Stickney, Boston, Lincolnshire
Telephone Nº: (01205) 723069
Year Formed: 2002
Location of Line: Stickney, off the A16
Length of Line: Over 1,500 metres of 7¼ inch gauge and 400 metres of 5 inch gauge

Nº of Steam Locos: 20
Nº of Other Locos: 15
Nº of Members: 50
Approx Nº of Visitors P.A.: Not known
Gauge: 5 inches and 7¼ inches
Web site: www.evergreens.net46.net

GENERAL INFO

Nearest Mainline Station:
Boston (10 miles)
Nearest Bus Station:
Boston (10 miles)
Car Parking: Available on site
Coach Parking: None
Food & Drinks: Available

SPECIAL INFORMATION

The site of the railway was previously a Horticultural Nursery and is around 3 acres in size. The site currently has no fewer than 3 level crossings, 3 bridges and 2 ponds!

OPERATING INFO

Opening Times: The last Saturday of each month from April to October. Trains run from 10.30am to 4.00pm.
Steam Working: Most operating days.
Prices:
Admission £2.00 (unlimited rides)
Family tickets £5.00 (unlimited rides)

Detailed Directions by Car:
The railway is situated on the A16 between Boston and Spilsby. Upon reaching the village of Stickney, look out for the signal on the grass verge which marks the entrance to the railway.

FENLAND LIGHT RAILWAY

Address: Mereside Farm, Mereside Drove, Ramsey Mereside, Cambs.	**Nº of Steam Locos**: 3+
Telephone Nº: None	**Nº of Other Locos**: 2+
Year Formed: 1991	**Nº of Members**: 12
Location of Line: Mereside Farm	**Approx Nº of Visitors P.A.**: 500 – 1,000
Length of Line: 800 feet	**Gauge**: 7¼ inches
	Web site: www.fenlandlightrailway.co.uk

GENERAL INFORMATION

Nearest Mainline Station: Peterborough (10 miles)
Nearest Bus Station: Peterborough (10 miles)
Car Parking: Available on site
Coach Parking: None
Food & Drinks: Available

SPECIAL INFORMATION

The railway is operated by volunteers from the Ramsey Miniature Steam Railway Society. The Society undertakes running days at local school fetes, country fairs and charity events by prior arrangement using up to 600 feet of portable track.

OPERATING INFORMATION

Opening Times: The third Sunday of each month from March to November inclusive except for August when two days are spent at the nearby Ramsey Rural Museum Fair which was formerly held at RAF Upwood. Santa Special running days usually take place on dates during December (pre-booking required). Please check the railway's website for further information.
Steam Working: All operating days.
Prices: From £1.00 per ride

Detailed Directions by Car:
From Ramsey: Travel up Great Whyte, turn right at the mini-roundabout by the Mill Apartments and follow onto Stocking Fen Road. Follow this road for just over a mile then turn left into Bodsey Toll Road for Ramsey Mereside. Follow this road until the signpost for Ramsey Mereside and turn right into Mereside Drove. The railway is on the left after approximately 1 mile.

FRIMLEY LODGE MINIATURE RAILWAY

Address: Frimley Lodge Park, Sturt Road, Frimley Green, Surrey GU16 6HT
Phone Nº: 07710 606461 (Please use on operating days only)
Year Formed: 1991
Location of Line: Frimley Green
Length of Line: 1 kilometre

Nº of Steam Locos: 5 (Members' locos)
Nº of Other Locos: 3
Nº of Members: Approximately 60
Approx Nº of Visitors P.A.: 20,000+
Gauge: 3½ inches, 5 inches & 7¼ inches
Web site: www.flmr.org

GENERAL INFORMATION

Nearest Mainline Station: Frimley or Ashvale (both 2 miles)
Nearest Bus Station: Farnborough (4 miles) – Take the Number 3 bus between Aldershot and Yately.
Car Parking: Available on site
Coach Parking: Available by prior arrangement
Food & Drinks: Cafe in the Park

SPECIAL INFORMATION

The Railway is operated by volunteers from the Frimley and Ascot Locomotive Club who bring their own Locomotives to give pleasure to others. All the proceeds are used for the maintenance of the Railway and to benefit local charities.

OPERATING INFORMATION

Opening Times: The first Sunday of the month from March to November. Also on August Bank Holiday and Wednesdays during the school holidays (subject to staff availability). Trains run from 11.00am to 5.00pm on Sundays and from 11.00am – 1.00pm then 2.00pm – 4.00pm on Wednesdays during the school holidays.
Steam Working: Operational Sundays only.
Prices: Single Rides £1.00
          Double Rides £1.20

Detailed Directions by Car:
Exit the M3 at Junction 4 and take the A331 towards Guildford. Leave the A331 at the turn-off for Mytchett and turn left at the top of the ramp then left again at the Miners Arms into Sturt Road. Cross over the bridge then turn right into Frimley Lodge Park. Once in the Park turn right then right again then take the next left for the Railway.

GOLDING SPRING MINIATURE RAILWAY

Address: Quainton Road Station,
Quainton, Aylesbury, Bucks.   HP22 4BY
Phone Nº: (01296) 623540 (Secretary)
Year Formed: 1972
Location: Within the Buckinghamshire
Railway Centre site
Length of Line: 1,200 yards

Nº of Steam Locos: 12
Nº of Other Locos: 4
Nº of Members: Approximately 120
Approx Nº of Visitors P.A.: 25,000
Gauge: 3½ inches, 5 inches & 7¼ inches
Web site: www.vames.org.uk

GENERAL INFORMATION

Nearest Mainline Station: Aylesbury (6 miles)
Nearest Bus Station: Aylesbury (6 miles)
Car Parking: Free parking for 500 cars available
Coach Parking: Free parking for 10 coaches
Souvenir Shop(s): Yes
Food & Drinks: Yes

SPECIAL INFORMATION

The Golding Spring Miniature Railway is operated
by members of the Vale of Aylesbury Model
Engineering Society and is located at the
Buckinghamshire Railway Centre. Other attractions
include a 32mm and 45mm Garden Railway.

OPERATING INFORMATION

Opening Times: Sundays and Bank Holidays from
March to October inclusive. Also on Wednesdays in
the school holidays to coincide with the Bucks
Railway Centre. Trains run from 10.30am to 5.30pm
Steam Working: Every operational day.
Prices: £1.00 per ride
         Under-3s travel free of charge

Detailed Directions by Car:
The Buckinghamshire Railway Centre is signposted off the A41 Aylesbury to Bicester Road at Waddesdon and off
the A413 Buckingham to Aylesbury road at Whitchurch. Junctions 7, 8 and 9 of the M40 are all close by.

GREAT COCKCROW RAILWAY

Address: Hardwick Lane, Lyne,
near Chertsey, Surrey KT16 0AD
Telephone Nº: (01932) 565474 (Sundays)
Year Formed: 1968
Location of Line: Lyne, near Chertsey
Length of Line: 2 miles

Nº of Steam Locos: Approximately 25
Nº of Other Locos: 3
Approx Nº of Visitors P.A.: 10,000
Gauge: 7¼ inches
Web site: www.cockcrow.co.uk

GENERAL INFORMATION

Nearest Mainline Station: Chertsey (30 min. walk)
Nearest Bus Stop: Chertsey (30 minute walk)
Car Parking: Available on site
Coach Parking: Limited parking available on site
Souvenir Shop(s): None
Food & Drinks: Available

SPECIAL INFORMATION

Emanating from the Greywood Central Railway,
built from 1946, at a private address in Walton-on-
Thames, the Great Cockcrow Railway opened in
1968 and has continually grown since moving to its
present site. The Railway offers a choice of two
regular routes, each served every few minutes.

OPERATING INFORMATION

Opening Times: 2013 dates: Sundays from 5th May
to 27th October when trains run from 1.30pm to
4.45pm. Also open on Wednesdays in August
(1.00pm to 4.00pm) and on 26th October (5.00pm
to 8.00pm).
Steam Working: Every operating day.
Prices: Various combinations of tickets are
available ranging from £3.50 for an ordinary adult
return to £17.50 for a family double return.

Detailed Directions by Car:
Exit the M25 at Junction 11 and take the A320 towards Woking. At the first roundabout take the exit towards
Chertsey and continue along this road passing St. Peter's Hospital on the left, then turn next left (B386) towards
Windlesham. Turn right almost immediately into Hardwick Lane and the railway on the right after about ¼ mile
just after Hardwick Farm.   Satellite Navigation: KT16 0AD

GRIMSBY & CLEETHORPES M.E.S.

Address: Waltham Windmill, Brigsley Road, Waltham, Grimsby   DN32 0JZ
Telephone Nº: None
Year Formed: 1985
Location: Waltham, near Grimsby
Length of Line: 1,300 feet for 7¼ and 5 inch gauges, 600 feet for 3½ gauge

Nº of Steam Locos: 1 (+ members' locos)
Nº of Other Locos: 2
Nº of Members: Approximately 80
Approx Nº of Visitors P.A.: Not known
Gauge: 3½ inches, 5 inches & 7¼ inches
Web site: www.gcmes.org.uk

GENERAL INFORMATION

Nearest Mainline Station: Grimsby (3 miles)
Nearest Bus Station: Grimsby (3 miles)
Car Parking: Available on site
Coach Parking: None
Food & Drinks: Available at the Windmill

SPECIAL INFORMATION

The Society's track is based in Waltham, near Grimsby adjacent to a preserved windmill dating back to 1878 which still operates from time to time.

OPERATING INFORMATION

Opening Times: 2013 dates: Sundays and Bank Holidays from 31st March to the end of September inclusive. Trains run from 12.00pm to 4.00pm.
Steam Working: Most operating days.
Prices: From 50p per ride

Detailed Directions by Car:
The Railway is situated by Waltham Windmill on the B1203 Grimsby to Binbrook Road and is well signposted. The B1203 connects to the A16 at Scartho, a suburb of Grimsby, about a mile from the railway or to the A18 at Ashby Top, about 3 miles away.

GUILDFORD M.E.S. RAILWAY

Address: Burchatts Farm, Stoke Park, Guildford, Surrey GU1 1TU
Telephone Nº: None
Year Formed: 1954
Location of Line: Stoke Park, Guildford
Length of Line: 990 feet ground level track and 1,405 feet raised track

Nº of Steam Locos: 6 + visiting locos
Nº of Other Locos: 1
Nº of Members: Over 200
Approx Nº of Visitors P.A.: 10,000
Gauges: 7¼ inches, 5 inches, 3½ inches and 2½ inches
Web site: www.gmes.org.uk

GENERAL INFO

Nearest Mainline Station:
Guildford London Road (½ mile)
Nearest Bus Station:
Guildford (2½ miles)
Car Parking: Street parking + some available on site
Coach Parking:
Street parking only
Souvenir Shop(s): None
Food & Drinks: Available

SPECIAL INFO

The Guildford Model Engineering Society has operated a railway at the Burchatts Farm site since 1958 and a 'Garden railway' also operates on site.

OPERATING INFO

Opening Times:
2013 Dates: 17th March, 21st April, 19th May, 16th June, 28th July, 18th August, 22nd September and 20th October – open from 2.00pm to 5.00pm on these dates. Also open for a Model Steam Rally and Exhibition on 20th & 21st July from 11.00am to 5.00pm.
Steam Working: Every open day.
Prices: 3 rides for £2.00
Admission prices for the Steam Rally: Adults £8.00
Under-16s Free of charge
Senior Citizens £6.00
(Note: The above prices may be subject to change).

Detailed Directions by Car:
The Railway is located at the Eastern end of Stoke Park in Guildford, not far from the Spectrum Sports Centre and near to the junction of the A25 (Parkway) and the A3100 (London Road). Access to the Burchatts Farm site is via London Road.

HALTON MINIATURE RAILWAY

Address: Town Park, Runcorn WA7 6PT
Telephone Nº: (01928) 701965
Year Formed: 1979
Location of Line: Runcorn
Length of Line: 1 mile approximately

Nº of Steam Locos: Members locos only
Nº of Other Locos: 4
Nº of Members: Approximately 25
Annual Membership Fee: £11.00
Approx Nº of Visitors P.A.: 12,500
Gauge: 7¼ inches
Website: www.haltonminiaturerailway.co.uk

GENERAL INFORMATION

Nearest Mainline Station: Runcorn East (¾ mile)
Nearest Bus Station: Runcorn (¾ mile)
Car Parking: Available on site
Coach Parking: Available
Souvenir Shop(s): None
Food & Drinks: Available at the adjacent Ski Centre

SPECIAL INFORMATION

The railway is operated by the Halton Miniature Railway Society and one of their locomotives, the Norton Priory (illustrated above), was built by schoolchildren from Norton Priory Secondary School in 1983! It has recently been restored to its former glory and is again in regular service.

OPERATING INFORMATION

Opening Times: Sundays throughout the year (weather permitting) from 1.00pm to 4.30pm.
Steam Working: Occasional dates only. Please contact the railway for further details.
Prices: Adults £1.00
Children £1.00

Detailed Directions by Car:
From All Parts: Exit the M56 at Junction 11 and follow the brown tourist signs for the Ski Centre which is adjacent to the railway.

HEMSWORTH WATER PARK MINIATURE RAILWAY

Address: Hoyle Mill Road, Kinsley, Pontefract WF9 5JB
Telephone Nº: (01977) 617617
Year Formed: 1995
Location of Line: Hemsworth Water Park
Length of Line: 300 yards
Web site: www.hemsworthcouncil.co.uk/waterpark.shtml

Nº of Steam Locos: None
Nº of Other Locos: 2
Approx Nº of Visitors P.A.: 60,000 (visitors to the Park); 6,500 journeys
Gauge: 7¼ inches

GENERAL INFORMATION

Nearest Mainline Station: Fitzwilliam (½ mile)
Nearest Bus Station: Hemsworth (½ mile)
Car Parking: Available on site
Coach Parking: Available
Souvenir Shop(s): None
Food & Drinks: Available at the Lakeside Cafe

SPECIAL INFORMATION

The railway is located at Hemsworth Water Park inside the Playworld by an adventure playground.

OPERATING INFORMATION

Opening Times: Weekends and School Holidays from Easter until early September from 10.00am to 6.00pm.
Steam Working: None at present.
Prices: Adults £1.00
         Children £1.00

Detailed Directions by Car:
From All Parts: The Park is located by the side of the B6273, just south of Kinsley and to the north of Hemsworth.

HIGH LEGH RAILWAY

Address: High Legh Garden Centre,
Halliwells Brow, High Legh WA16 0QW
Telephone Nº: 07799 118968
Year Formed: 2009
Location of Line: High Legh, Cheshire
Length of Line: 900 yards

Nº of Steam Locos: 1
Nº of Other Locos: 6
Approx Nº of Visitors P.A.: 10,000
Gauge: 7¼ inches
Web site:
www.cheshirerailways.co.uk/highlegh

GENERAL INFORMATION

Nearest Mainline Station: Knutsford (6 miles)
Nearest Bus Station: Warrington (9 miles)
Car Parking: Available on site
Coach Parking: Available
Souvenir Shop(s): Yes
Food & Drinks: Available

SPECIAL INFORMATION

In addition to rides, the railway also offers driving
experience events from time to time. Contact the
railway for further details.

OPERATING INFORMATION

Opening Times: Weekends, Bank Holidays and
daily during School Holidays throughout the year.
Open 10.30am to 4.30pm.
Steam Working: Please check the web site for
further information.
Prices: Adults £1.00
Children £1.00 (Toddlers ride free)

Detailed Directions by Car:
From All Parts: Exit the M6 at Junction 20 and take the A50 towards Knutsford following signs for Poplar Services.
High Legh Garden Centre is located to the south of the A50 in High Legh.

HILCOTE VALLEY RAILWAY

Address: Fletchers Garden Centre,
Bridge Farm, Stone Road, Eccleshall,
ST21 6JY
Telephone Nº: (01785) 284553
Year Formed: 1993
Location of Line: Eccleshall, Staffordshire
Length of Line: 500 yards

Nº of Steam Locos: 3
Nº of Other Locos: 2
Approx Nº of Visitors P.A.: 5,000+
Gauge: 7¼ inches
Web site:
www.hilcotevalleyrailway.webs.com

GENERAL INFORMATION

Nearest Mainline Station: Stafford (6 miles)
Nearest Bus Station: Stafford (6 miles)
Car Parking: Available on site
Coach Parking: Available
Souvenir Shop(s): None
Food & Drinks: Available on site

SPECIAL INFORMATION

Railway enthusiast Roger Greatrex designed and
built this railway himself!

OPERATING INFORMATION

Opening Times: Weekends and Bank Holidays
from Good Friday to the end of October from
11.30am to 5.00pm (from 1.00pm to 5.00pm on
Saturdays). Also open on afternoons during the
School Holidays, 1.00pm to 4.30pm.
Steam Working: Sundays only.
Prices: Adults £1.00
          Children £1.00

Detailed Directions by Car:
From All Parts: Exit the M6 at Junction 14 and take the A5013 to Eccleshall. Just after the junction with the A519,
turn right onto the B5026 Stone Road and the Garden Centre is on the right at Bridge Farm after ¾ mile.

HOLLYBUSH MINIATURE RAILWAY

Address: Hollybush Garden Centre, Warstone Road, Shareshill, Wolverhampton   WV10 7LX
Telephone Nº: (01922) 418050
Year Formed: 1996
Location of Line: Wolverhampton
Length of Line: 950 yards

Nº of Steam Locos: None
Nº of Other Locos: 2
Approx Nº of Visitors P.A.: Not known
Gauge: 7¼ inches
Web site: www.hollybush-garden.com/miniature-railway/

GENERAL INFORMATION

Nearest Mainline Station: Cannock (4 miles)
Nearest Bus Station: Cannock (4 miles)
Car Parking: Available on site
Coach Parking: Available
Souvenir Shop(s): Yes
Food & Drinks: Available

OPERATING INFORMATION

Opening Times: Wednesday to Sunday from Easter to early September and daily during the School Holidays. Also weekends from September to Christmas. Trains run from 10.30am to 4.30pm.
Steam Working: None at present.
Prices: Adults £1.50
            Children £1.50 (Under-2s ride free)

Detailed Directions by Car:
From All Parts: Exit the M6 at Junction 11 and follow the brown tourist signs onto the A462 for the railway which is on the left after approximately 600 yards.

HOLLYCOMBE – STEAM IN THE COUNTRY

Address: Iron Hill, Midhurst Road,
Liphook, Hants. GU30 7LP
Telephone Nº: (01428) 724900
Year Formed: 1971
Location of Line: Hollycombe, Liphook
Length of Line: 1¾ miles Narrow gauge,
¼ mile Standard gauge, 1,400 yards 7¼
inch gauge

Nº of Steam Locos: 6
Nº of Other Locos: 2
Nº of Members: 75
Annual Membership Fee: £10.00
Approx Nº of Visitors P.A.: 25,000
Gauge: 2 feet, Standard & 7¼ inches
Web site: www.hollycombe.co.uk

GENERAL INFORMATION

Nearest Mainline Station: Liphook (1 mile)
Nearest Bus Station: Liphook
Car Parking: Extensive grass area
Coach Parking: Hardstanding
Souvenir Shop(s): Yes
Food & Drinks: Yes – Cafe

SPECIAL INFORMATION

The narrow gauge railway ascends to spectacular
views of the Downs and is part of an extensive
working steam museum.

OPERATING INFORMATION

Opening Times: 2013 dates: Sundays and Bank
Holidays from Easter until the 13th October.
Steam Working: Please contact the museum for
further information.
Prices: Adult £13.00
Child £10.00
Senior Citizen £10.00
Family £40.00 (2 adults + 2 children)
Family £50.00 (2 adults + 3 children)

Detailed Directions by Car:
Take the A3 to Liphook and follow the brown tourist signs for the museum.

HULL & DISTRICT S.M.E.E.

Address: c/o West Park Bowls Pavilion, Walton Street, Hull   HU5 6JU
Phone Nº: (01262) 678767 (Secretary)
Year Formed: 1937
Location of Line: West Park, Hull
Length of Line: 190 metres (raised track) and 400 metres (ground level track)
Web site: www.finnaj.karoo.net/hdsmee.html

Nº of Steam Locos: Approximately 15
Nº of Other Locos: Approximately 10
Nº of Members: Approximately 68
Approx Nº of Visitors P.A.: 5,000
Gauge: 2½ inches, 3½ inches & 5 inches on the raised track; 5 inches & 7¼ inches on the ground level track

GENERAL INFORMATION

Nearest Mainline Station: Hull Paragon (1½ miles)
Nearest Bus Station: Hull Central (1½ miles)
Car Parking: Available on site
Coach Parking: None
Food & Drinks: None

SPECIAL INFORMATION

The Hull & District Society of Model & Experimental Engineers operates a railway in West Park in Hull.

OPERATING INFORMATION

Opening Times: Passenger services run on Sundays from noon until teatime subject to demand levels and the season. The railway also runs on some Wednesday afternoons during the school holidays. Please contact the railway for further information.
Steam Working: Whenever available.
Prices: Train rides are 30p per person but additional donations are also welcomed.

Detailed Directions by Car:
From the West, take the M62 to Hull where it becomes the A63. Continue along the A63 (Clive Sullivan Way) then turn left into Rawling Way following the signs for Hull Royal Infirmary. After ½ mile turn left onto Anlaby Road (A1105) then right after ½ mile into Walton Street. Turn right into West Park then right again for the Railway.

ILFORD & WEST ESSEX MODEL RAILWAY CLUB

Address: Station Road, Chadwell Heath, Romford, Essex	**N⁰ of Steam Locos**: 3
	N⁰ of Other Locos: 2
Telephone N⁰: (01708) 450424	**N⁰ of Members**: Approximately 50
Year Formed: 1930	**Approx N⁰ of Visitors P.A.**: 400
Location of Line: Chadwell Heath	**Gauge**: 7¼ inches
Length of Line: 150 yards	**Web site**: www.iwemrc.org.uk

GENERAL INFORMATION

Nearest Mainline Station: Chadwell Heath
Nearest Bus Station: Chadwell Heath (100 yards)
Car Parking: None on site but a public car park is 100 yards away
Coach Parking: None
Food & Drinks: Light refreshments are available

SPECIAL INFORMATION

The Ilford & West Essex Model Railway Club was formed in 1930 and as such is one of the oldest clubs of its type in the country. Please note that access to the site is by steps only and it is therefore not suitable for wheelchairs.

OPERATING INFORMATION

Opening Times: 2013 dates: The first Sunday of the month from May to September inclusive. Please contact the railway for further information. Trains run from 10.30am to 4.00pm.
Steam Working: All operating days.
Prices: 50p per ride or £3.00 for an all-day pass

Detailed Directions by Car:
The site is alongside Chadwell Heath mainline station just off the A118 between Romford and Ilford town centres. Station Road is to the South of the A118 approximately half-way between the two towns. The site itself is approximately 200 yards down Station Road with a car park on the right hand side.

KING'S LYNN & DISTRICT S.M.E.

Address: Lynnsport, Green Park Avenue, King's Lynn, Norfolk   PE30 2NB
Telephone Nº: 0796 309-3270
Year Formed: 1972
Location of Line: King's Lynn
Length of Line: 627 feet

Nº of Steam Locos: 8
Nº of Other Locos: 14
Nº of Members: 52
Annual Membership Fee: £18.00 Adult
Approx Nº of Visitors P.A.: 1,200
Gauge: 3½ inches, 5 inches & 7¼ inches
Web site: www.kldsme.org.uk

GENERAL INFORMATION

Nearest Mainline Station: King's Lynn (1 mile)
Nearest Bus Station: King's Lynn (1 mile)
Car Parking: Available on site
Coach Parking: Available
Food & Drinks: Available in Lynnsport

SPECIAL INFORMATION

The King's Lynn & District Society of Model Engineers first operated a railway in 1972 and the current track at Lynnsport has been working since 1992. Improvements to the Lynnsport facilities have been ongoing ever since.

OPERATING INFORMATION

Opening Times: Every Sunday from Easter until the end of October. Trains run from 1.00pm to 5.00pm
Steam Working: Most operating days.
Prices: 50p per ride.

Detailed Directions by Car:
Lynnsport is well-signposted from the outskirts of King's Lynn so it is easy to find just by following the signs. The railway itself is signposted once in the Lynnsport car park.

KINVER & WEST MIDLANDS S.M.E.

Correspondence: 24 Goodrest Avenue, Halesowen, West Midlands B62 0HP
Telephone Nº: (0121) 602-2019
Year Formed: 1961
Location of Line: Marsh Playing Fields, Kinver, Staffordshire
Length of Line: ½ mile

Nº of Steam Locos: Members locos only
Nº of Other Locos: Members locos only
Nº of Members: Approximately 100
Approx Nº of Visitors P.A.: Not known
Gauge: 3½ inches and 5 inches
Website: www.kinvermodelengineers.org.uk

GENERAL INFORMATION

Nearest Mainline Station: Kidderminster (6 miles)
Nearest Bus Station: Stourbridge (3 miles)
Car Parking: Available on site
Coach Parking: Available on site
Food & Drinks: None

SPECIAL INFORMATION

The Kinver & West Midlands Society of Model Engineers dates back to organisations formed in the 1920s and has operated a railway in Kinver since 1962. In addition to the main 3½ and 5 inch line, a short 7¼ inch track is now in operation at the site.

OPERATING INFORMATION

Opening Times: Sunday afternoons between Easter and October, weather permitting. Trains run between 2.00pm and 5.00pm.
Steam Working: Most operating days.
Prices: £1.00 per ride.

Detailed Directions by Car:
The Society's tracksite is situated on the Marsh Playing Fields at the end of the High Street in the village of Kinver which is to the West of Stourbridge and to the North of Kidderminster.

LANGFORD & BEELEIGH RAILWAY

Address: Museum of Power, Hatfield Road, Langford, Maldon, Essex, CM9 6QA **Telephone Nº**: (01621) 843183 **Year Formed**: 2003 **Length of Line**: ¼ mile loop	**Nº of Steam Locos**: 4 **Nº of Other Locos**: 1 **Nº of Members**: Approximately 140 **Approx Nº of Visitors P.A.**: 6,000 **Gauge**: 7¼ inches **Web site**: www.museumofpower.org.uk

GENERAL INFORMATION

Nearest Mainline Station: Witham (4 miles)
Nearest Bus Station: Chelmsford (6 miles)
Car Parking: Available on site
Coach Parking: Available
Souvenir Shop(s): Yes
Food & Drinks: Available

SPECIAL INFORMATION

The Railway is situated at the Museum of Power which is housed in the Steam Pumping Station at Langford in Essex. The Museum was set up to exhibit and demonstrate working examples of power sources of all types and chronicle the major roles that they have played in history.

OPERATING INFORMATION

Opening Times: 2013 dates: 17th & 31st March; 21st April; 5th & 19th May; 2nd & 16th June; 7th July; 4th August; 8th and 15th September; 6th October; 8th December for pre-booked Santa Specials plus an event on 1st January 2014. Please contact the Museum for further information.
Steam Working: On all operating days.
Prices: £1.00 per ride (6 rides for £5.00)
Note: Admission to the Museum is an extra charge.

Detailed Directions by Car:
The Museum is situated in Langford, on the B1019 Maldon to Hatfield Peverel Road. From the A12, take the Hatfield Peverel exit, pass through the village and take the B1019 Hatfield Road towards Ulting & Maldon. The Museum is on the right hand side after approximately 3 miles on the outskirts of Langford.

LEICESTER SOCIETY OF MODEL ENGINEERS

Address: Abbey Park, Leicester LE1 3EJ	**Nº of Steam Locos**: Members locos only
Telephone Nº: (0116) 247-9844	**Nº of Other Locos**: 5 diesels
Year Formed: 1909	**Nº of Members**: 100+
Location of Line: Victorian Public Park	**Annual Membership Fee**: £30.00
Length of Line: 874 yards	**Approx Nº of Visitors P.A.**: 7,500+
Web site: None at present	**Gauges**: 2½ inches, 3½ inches, 5 inches
E-mail: eva.day@btinternet.com	and 7¼ inches

GENERAL INFORMATION

Nearest Mainline Station: Leicester (1½ miles)
Nearest Bus Station: Leicester (½ mile)
Car Parking: Available on site
Coach Parking: None
Souvenir Shop(s): None
Food & Drinks: None, but available elsewhere in the Park

SPECIAL INFORMATION

The Society has been located within Abbey Park since 1953.

OPERATING INFORMATION

Opening Times: 2013 dates: Sundays, Bank Holidays and occasional Wednesdays from Easter until the 27th October. Trains run from 1.00pm to 5.00pm. Santa Specials will run on 8th December.
Steam Working: Subject to availability.
Prices: Adults £1.00
Children £1.00 (Under-5s ride for free)
Family Ticket £3.00 (2 adults + 3 children)

Detailed Directions by Car:
From All Parts: The railway is located at the South-Western edge of Leicester's Abbey Park. Take the inner ring road to St. Margaret's Bus Station and vehicular access to the park is by the nearby Slater Street entrance (off St.Margaret's Way).

Littledown Miniature Railway

Address: Littledown Park, Chaseside, Castle Lane East, Bournemouth, BH7 7DX
Contact Telephone Nº: 07879 355399
Year Formed: 1924
Location of Line: Littledown Park
Length of Line: Over one third of a mile

Nº of Steam Locos: 15+
Nº of Other Locos: 10+
Nº of Members: 140+
Approx Nº of Visitors P.A.: 4,000
Gauge: 3½ inches, 5 inches & 7¼ inches
Web site: www.littledownrailway.co.uk

GENERAL INFORMATION

Nearest Mainline Station: Bournemouth Central (3½ miles)
Nearest Bus Station: Bournemouth
Car Parking: In Littledown Leisure Centre car park
Coach Parking: As above

SPECIAL INFORMATION

Bournemouth and District Society of Model Engineers operate the railway at Littledown Park. The society also operates a 16mm garden railway alongside the track.

OPERATING INFO

Opening Times: Most Sundays and Wednesdays throughout the year subject to weather conditions. Trains run from 11.00am to 3.00pm.
Steam Working: Subject to availability. Please contact the railway for further information.
Prices: £1.00 per ride.

Detailed Directions by Car:
The Railway is situated at Littledown Park which is to the North-East of Bournemouth town centre close (and to the South of) the junction of Wessex Way (A338) and Castle Lane (A3060).

LITTLE HAY MINIATURE RAILWAY

Address: Balleny Green, Little Hay Lane, Little Hay WS14 0QA
Telephone N°: (0121) 308-6886
Year Formed: 1948
Location of Line: To the North of Little Hay Hamlet
Length of Line: ½ mile (Ground level)

N° of Steam Locos: 20 (approximately)
N° of Other Locos: 4
N° of Members: Approximately 105
Approx N° of Visitors P.A.: 4,500
Gauge: 2½ inches, 3½ inches, 5 inches and 7¼ inches (elevated & ground level)
Web site: www.scmes.co.uk

GENERAL INFORMATION

Nearest Mainline Station: Blake Street (1½ miles)
Nearest Bus Station: Sutton Coldfield or Lichfield (each approximately 5 miles)
Car Parking: Available on site
Coach Parking: None
Food & Drinks: Drinks available at all times with food available at some special events

SPECIAL INFORMATION

The Railway is owned and operated by members of the Sutton Coldfield Model Engineering Society Ltd. and has been based at Balleny Green since 1981.

The site has been progressively developed since this date. The number and types of locomotives in operation depends on those provided by attending members.

OPERATING INFORMATION

Opening Times: Some Saturdays, Sundays and Bank Holidays throughout the year. Also at various other dates. Please contact the Society or check their web site for further details.
Steam Working: All operating days.
Prices: Prices depend on the event being held.

Detailed Directions by Car:
From the A38/A5 Junction: Head south on the A38 dual carriageway and turn right at the sign for Little Hay. Follow the road past the Pumping Station and Holly Bush pub then turn left after approximately 100 yards through the steel gates set between stone pillars with lanterns to enter the railway.

LLWYFAN CERRIG MINIATURE RAILWAY

Address: c/o Gwili Railway, Bronwydd Arms SA33 6HT
Telephone No: (01267) 238213
Year Formed: 1993
Location of Line: Llwyfan Cerrig Station on the Gwili Railway
Length of Line: 300 yards

No of Steam Locos: None
No of Other Locos: 1
No of Members: 900 shareholders, 450 Society members (Gwili Railway)
Annual Membership Fee: £15.00
Approx No of Visitors P.A.: 28,000
Gauge: 7¼ inches
Web site: www.gwili-railway.co.uk

GENERAL INFORMATION

Nearest Mainline Station: Carmarthen (3 miles)
Nearest Bus Station: Carmarthen (3 miles)
Car Parking: Free parking at Bronwydd Arms
Coach Parking: Free parking at Bronwydd Arms
Souvenir Shop(s): Yes
Food & Drinks: Yes

SPECIAL INFORMATION

The railway can only be reached via the standard-gauge Gwili Railway line. The cost of rides on the miniature railway are included in the standard gauge railway fares!

OPERATING INFORMATION

Opening Times: Bank Holidays from April, some other dates in May then Tuesday to Thursday and Sundays in June and July. Daily in August. Open most weekends in September and December. Also open on certain other dates. Please phone or check the website for further details.
Steam Working: None at present
Prices: Adult £9.00
Child £3.00 (Under-2s ride for free)
Senior Citizens £8.00
Note: The above prices are for rides on the standard gauge Gwili Railway. Miniature Railway rides are included in these prices.

Detailed Directions by Car:
Gwili Railway is three miles North of Carmarthen – signposted off the A484 Carmarthen to Cardigan Road. The Llwyfan Cerrig Miniature Railway is only accessible via the Gwili Railway Line.

MILTON KEYNES LIGHT RAILWAY

Address: Caldecotte Arms, Bletcham Way, Milton Keynes MK7 8HP	**N° of Steam Locos**: 4
Telephone N°: (01908) 503889	**N° of Other Locos**: 2
Year Formed: 1972	**N° of Members**: 40
Location: Caldecotte Arms, Milton Keynes	**Annual Membership Fee**: £35.00 Adult
Length of Line: 280 metres (raised track) and 300 metres (ground level)	**Approx N° of Visitors P.A.**: 2,000
	Gauge: 3½ inches, 5 inches and 7¼ inches
	Web site: www.mklightrailway.co.uk

GENERAL INFORMATION

Nearest Mainline Station: Milton Keynes Central (3 miles)
Nearest Bus Station: Milton Keynes Central
Car Parking: Available on site
Coach Parking: Available on site
Souvenir Shop(s): None
Food & Drinks: Available at the Caldecotte Arms

SPECIAL INFORMATION

The MK Light Railway is operated by members of the Milton Keynes Model Engineering Society. The Society recently began construction of a ground level track for 5 inch and 7¼ inch gauge engines. The first stage of 300 metres has been completed and further extensions are planned to take the line to 1¼ miles in length.

OPERATING INFORMATION

Opening Times: Every Sunday from April to September from 12.00pm to 4.00pm. Open the first Sunday of the month from October through to February subject to weather conditions, also from 12.00pm to 4.00pm.
Steam Working: Most operating days.
Prices: £1.00 per person (twice round the track)

Detailed Directions by Car:
From the North: Exit the M1 at Junction 13 and take the A421 into Milton Keynes. At the 2nd roundabout, turn left into Tongwell Street (A4146). Continue along this road then turn right at the 2nd roundabout into Bletcham Way, go straight on at the next roundabout and turn back on yourself at the following roundabout and the Caldecotte Arms is on the left and easy to see with a replica Windmill as part of the building!
From the South: Exit the M1 at Junction 9 and follow the A5 for approximately 15 miles into Milton Keynes. Turn off the A5 onto the A4146 Bletcham Way and the Caldecotte Arms is on the left after a short distance.

MOORS VALLEY RAILWAY

Address: Moors Valley Country Park, Horton Road, Ashley Heath, Nr. Ringwood, Hants. BH24 2ET
Telephone Nº: (01425) 471415
Year Formed: 1985
Location: Moors Valley Country Park

Length of Line: 1 mile
Nº of Steam Locos: 15
Nº of Other Locos: 2
Approx Nº of Visitors P.A.: 100,000
Gauge: 7¼ inches
Web site: www.moorsvalleyrailway.co.uk

GENERAL INFORMATION

Nearest Mainline Station: Bournemouth (12 miles)
Nearest Bus Station: Ringwood (3 miles)
Car Parking: Parking charges vary throughout the year. Maximum charge £8.00 per day.
Coach Parking: Charges are applied for parking
Souvenir Shop(s): Yes + Model Railway Shop
Food & Drinks: Yes

SPECIAL INFORMATION

The Moors Valley Railway is a complete small Railway with signalling and 2 signal boxes and also 4 tunnels and 2 level crossings.

OPERATING INFORMATION

Opening Times: Weekends throughout the year. Daily from one week before to one week after Easter, Spring Bank Holiday to mid-September, during School half-term holidays and also from Boxing Day to end of School holidays. Also Santa Specials in December and occasional other openings. Phone the Railways for details.
Steam Working: 10.45am to 5.00pm when open.
Prices: Adult Return £3.45; Adult Single £2.30
Child Return £1.95; Child Single £1.45
Special rates are available for parties of 10 or more.

Detailed Directions by Car:
From All Parts: Moors Valley Country Park is situated on Horton Road which is off the A31 Ferndown to Ringwood road near the junction with the A338 to Bournemouth.

NESS ISLANDS RAILWAY

Address: Whin Park, Inverness IV3 5SS	**Nº of Steam Locos**: 1
Telephone Nº: (01463) 235533	**Nº of Other Locos**: 2
Year Formed: 1983	**Approx Nº of Visitors P.A.**: 12,000
Location of Line: Inverness	**Gauge**: 7¼ inches
Length of Line: 900 yards	**Web site**: www.nessislandsrailway.co.uk

GENERAL INFORMATION

Nearest Mainline Station: Inverness (2 miles)
Nearest Bus Station: Inverness (2 miles)
Car Parking: Available on site
Coach Parking: Available
Souvenir Shop(s): Yes
Food & Drinks: None

SPECIAL INFORMATION

Ness Islands Railway is Britain's most northerly 7¼ inch gauge line.

OPERATING INFORMATION

Opening Times: 2013 dates: Weekends from Easter to the end of October and also daily during the School Holidays. Trains run from 11.30am to 5.00pm.
Steam Working: Most weekends.
Prices: Adults £1.80 per ride
Children £1.80 per ride

Detailed Directions by Car:
From All Parts: The Railway is located in Inverness, just to the south of the A82 Glenurquhart Road. Turn into Bught Road at Queens Park and the railway is on the right after a short distance.

NORTH SCARLE MINIATURE RAILWAY

Address: North Scarle Playing Field, Swinderby Road, North Scarle, Lincolnshire   LN6 9ER (for Satnav)
Telephone Nº: (01522) 881760
Year Formed: 1933
Location of Line: North Scarle, between Newark and Lincoln
Length of Line: A third of a mile

Nº of Steam Locos: 7
Nº of Other Locos: 5
Nº of Members: 60
Annual Membership Fee: –
Approx Nº of Visitors P.A.: 3,000
Gauges: 7¼ inches and 5 inches

GENERAL INFORMATION

Nearest Mainline Station: Newark Northgate (5 miles)
Nearest Bus Station: Newark (5 miles)
Car Parking: 300 spaces available on site
Coach Parking: None available
Souvenir Shop(s): None
Food & Drinks: Available on special days only

SPECIAL INFORMATION

The Railway is owned and operated by the Lincoln and District Model Engineering Society which was founded in 1933.

OPERATING INFORMATION

Opening Times: Car Boot Sale Sundays only!
Dates for 2013: 31st March; 14th & 28th April; 12th & 26th May; 9rd & 23rd June; 7th & 21st July; 4th & 18th August; 1st, 15th & 29th September.
Trains run from 9.00am to 12.00pm.
Steam Working: Every running day.
Prices: Adult Return 80p
        Child Return 80p

Detailed Directions by Car:
North Scarle is situated off the A46 between Lincoln and Newark (about 5 miles from Newark). Alternatively, take the A1133 from Gainsborough and follow the North Scarle signs when around 6 miles from Newark.

NORTHAMPTON SOCIETY OF MODEL ENGINEERS

Contact Address: Hon. Secretary,
10 High Street, Blisworth   NN7 3BJ
Telephone Nº: 0790 705-1388
Year Formed: 1933
Location of Line: Lower Delapre Park,
London Road, Northampton
Length of Line: 1,740 feet (raised track)
and 3,034 feet (ground level track)

Nº of Steam Locos: Up to 9 running
Nº of Other Locos: 4 to 6 run occasionally
Nº of Members: 120
Approx Nº of Visitors P.A.: 10,000
Gauge: 3½ inches, 5 inches & 7¼ inches
Web site: www.nsme.co.uk

GENERAL INFORMATION

Nearest Mainline Station: Northampton (2 miles)
Nearest Bus Station: Northampton (2 miles)
Car Parking: Available on site
Coach Parking: On London Road
Food & Drinks: Light refreshments are available

SPECIAL INFORMATION

The Northampton Society of Model Engineers is a long established society with excellent facilities for model engineers. The society has over 120 members with wide ranging interests, several of whom have won major awards at National exhibitions.

The two tracks were extended during 2011 and are located in a woodland setting with a new garden railway and a picnic site. The site may be hired for Birthday parties on Tuesdays and Saturdays. Please check the web site for further information.

OPERATING INFORMATION

Opening Times: May Day Bank Holiday Monday then the first Sunday of the month thereafter up to and including October. Trains run from 2.00pm to 5.00pm.
Steam Working: Every operating day.
Prices: 50p per ride.

Detailed Directions by Car:
From the M1: Exit at Junction 15 and take the A508 to Northampton. Take the 2nd turn off onto the A45 (for the Town Centre) and then the 2nd exit at the roundabout. After ½ mile turn right just before the pelican crossing and immediately turn left through the steel gate onto the access track for the railway; From the East: Follow the A45 and take the turn off signposted for Daventry and the Town Centre. Take the 4th exit at the roundabout onto the A508, then as above; From the Town Centre: Take the A508 South (Bridge Street). Cross the river and go straight on at the traffic lights. Pass a petrol station on the left and immediately after the pelican crossing turn left then immediately left again for the railway.

NORWICH & DISTRICT S.M.E.

Correspondence Address: 'Timberlee', Bungay Road, Scole, Diss   IP21 4DX
Telephone Nº: (01379) 740578
Year Formed: 1933
Location of Line: Eaton Park, Norwich
Nº of Steam Locos: 5
Nº of Other Locos: 2

Length of Line: Two tracks – one of 800 metres (7¼ and 5 inch gauges) and one of 955 feet (5 and 3½ inch gauges)
Nº of Members: Approximately 120
Approx Nº of Visitors P.A.: 8,000
Gauge: 3½ inches, 5 inches & 7¼ inches
Web site: www.ndsme.co.uk

GENERAL INFORMATION

Nearest Mainline Station: Norwich (3 miles)
Nearest Bus Station: Norwich (2 miles)
Car Parking: Available in Eaton Park
Coach Parking: None
Food & Drinks: Available in Eaton Park

SPECIAL INFORMATION

Norwich & District Society of Model Engineers was formed in 1933 and operates two tracks in Eaton Park, one raised and the other ground level.

OPERATING INFORMATION

Opening Times: Sundays during the busy season. Trains run from 2.00pm to 5.00pm. Please contact the railway for further details.
Steam Working: Every operating day.
Prices: £1.00 per ride on the long track
(only open on alternating Sundays)
50p per ride on the short track

Detailed Directions by Car:
Take the A11 or A140 into Norwich and upon reaching the ring road, turn left. At the second set of traffic lights turn left into South Park Avenue and the entrance to Eaton Park is on the right hand side.
Alternative route: Take the A47 into Norwich and turn right at the ring road. At the 3rd set of traffic lights turn right into South Park Avenue.

ORCHID LINE MINIATURE RAILWAY

Address: Curraghs Wildlife Park, Ballaugh, Isle of Man
Telephone Nº: (01624) 880085
Year Formed: 1992
Location: Within the Wildlife Park
Length of Line: 1,000 yards

Nº of Steam Locos: 8
Nº of Other Locos: 3
Nº of Members: Approximately 75
Approx Nº of Visitors P.A.: 15,000
Gauge: 3½ inches, 5 inches & 7¼ inches
Web sites: www.gov.im/wildlife or www.homepages.mcb.net/howe/msmec.htm

GENERAL INFORMATION

Nearest Bus Station: At the Wildlife Park
Car Parking: Available on site
Coach Parking: Available
Souvenir Shop(s): Yes
Food & Drinks: Available

SPECIAL INFORMATION

The Railway is operated by members of the Manx Steam & Model Engineering Club. Please note that an entrance fee is charged to enter the Wildlife Park and this is required to access the railway.

OPERATING INFORMATION

Railway Opening Times: Sundays and Bank Holidays from Easter to October. Trains run from 12.00pm to 4.30pm.
Steam Working: Most operating days.
Prices: 80p per ride
Note: The above price does not include the entrance fee for the Wildlife Park.

Detailed Directions by Car:
Curraghs Wildlife Park lies on the main road between Ramsey and Ballaugh and is well-signposted.

PENTNEY PARK RAILWAY

Address: Pentney, King's Lynn, PE32 1HU
Telephone Nº: (01760) 337479
Year Formed: 1983
Location of Line: North-west Norfolk
Length of Line: 1 mile

Nº of Steam Locos: Visiting locos only
Nº of Other Locos: 2
Nº of Members: –
Approx Nº of Visitors P.A.: 10,000 (to the Park)
Gauge: 7¼ inches
Web site: www.pentney-park.co.uk

GENERAL INFORMATION

Nearest Mainline Station: King's Lynn (9 miles)
Nearest Bus Station: King's Lynn (9 miles)
Car Parking: Available on site
Coach Parking: Available
Souvenir Shop(s): None
Food & Drinks: None

SPECIAL INFORMATION

Close to Sandringham, the railway is located within the Pentney holiday and camping leisure park.

OPERATING INFORMATION

Opening Times: Selected weekends between the end of May and September. Please phone for further information.
Steam Working: Occasional visiting locos only.
Prices: £1.50 per ride

Detailed Directions by Car:
From All Parts: The Park is located just off the A47 between King's Lynn and Swaffham at the junction with the B1153.

PINEWOOD MINIATURE RAILWAY

Address: Pinewood Leisure Centre, Old Wokingham Road, Wokingham, Berkshire RG40 3AQ **Phone Nº**: None **Year Formed**: 1984 **Location**: Pinewood Leisure Centre **Length of Line**: 800 metres	**Nº of Steam Locos**: 30 (All owned **Nº of Other Locos**: 10 by Members) **Nº of Members**: Approximately 40 **Annual Membership Fee**: £35.00 **Approx Nº of Visitors P.A.**: 3,000 **Gauge**: 5 inches and 7¼ inches **Web site**: www.pinewoodrailway.co.uk

GENERAL INFORMATION

Nearest Mainline Station: Bracknell
Nearest Bus Station: Bracknell
Car Parking: Available on site
Coach Parking: Available by arrangement
Souvenir Shop(s): None
Food & Drinks: Tea/Coffee making facilities only

SPECIAL INFORMATION

The Pinewood Miniature Railway runs through attractive woodlands backing on to a Leisure Centre.

OPERATING INFORMATION

Opening Times: Public running on the 3rd Sunday in the month from April to October. Santa Specials on the first two Sundays in December (pre-booking is advised for these dates). Private Parties can sometimes be catered for by prior arrangement.
Steam Working: All open days.
Prices: £1.00 per ride or 6 rides for £5.00

Detailed Directions by Car:
From the M3 or the A30 take the A322 towards Bracknell. Once on the A322, keep in the left hand lane to the first major roundabout then take the first exit onto the B3430 towards Wokingham along Nine Mile Ride. Cross the next roundabout (A3095) and continue on the B3430 passing the Golden Retriever pub and the Crematorium. Go straight on at the next mini-roundabout then turn right at the following roundabout into Old Wokingham Road. The Pinewood Leisure Centre is on the left after approximately 100 metres.

PLYMOUTH MINIATURE STEAM

Address: Goodwin Park, Pendeen Crescent, Southway, Plymouth	**Nº of Steam Locos**: 2 + member locos
Phone Nº: (01752) 201771 (Secretary)	**Nº of Other Locos**: 2 + member locos
Year Formed: 1970	**Nº of Members**: Approximately 100
Location of Line: Goodwin Park Public Nature Reserve	**Approx Nº of Visitors P.A.**: 2,000
Length of Line: ½ mile	**Gauge**: 3½ inches, 5 inches & 7¼ inches
	Web site: www.plymouthminiaturesteam.co.uk

GENERAL INFORMATION

Nearest Mainline Station: Plymouth (6 miles)
Nearest Bus Station: Plymouth (6 miles)
Car Parking: Available on site
Coach Parking: None
Food & Drinks: Light refreshments available.

SPECIAL INFORMATION

The railway runs through Goodwin Park, a site specially developed by members of the Society which was opened in 1990 and has since been designated as a Public Nature Reserve.

OPERATING INFORMATION

Opening Times: Open during the 1st and 3rd Sunday afternoons of each month from April to October inclusive, from 2.00pm to 4.30pm.
Steam Working: Most operating days.
Prices: 50 per ride.

Detailed Directions by Car:

From the A38 Plymouth Parkway, follow the signs for Tavistock (A386) travelling North until reaching a new road junction near Plymouth Airport and a Park & Ride site. Turn left at this junction into the Southway Estate and follow the road for ½ mile past two mini-roundabouts and a set of traffic lights. At the 3rd mini-roundabout turn left into Pendeen Crescent and about 200 yard on the right is a signpost for the railway. Follow the lane to the parking area but please note that the bridge has just 6 feet headroom so large vehicles must park outside the track!

PORTERSWICK JUNCTION LIGHT RAILWAY

Address: Hidden Valley Discovery Park, Tredidon St. Thomas, Launceston, Cornwall PL15 8SJ
Telephone Nº: (01566) 86463
Year Formed: 2003
Location of Line: Near Launceston
Length of Line: 1 mile

Nº of Steam Locos: 1
Nº of Other Locos: 1
Approx Nº of Visitors P.A.: 10,000
Gauge: 7¼ inches
Web site: www.hiddenvalleydiscoverypark.co.uk

GENERAL INFORMATION

Nearest Mainline Station: Liskeard (16 miles)
Nearest Bus Station: Launceston (4 miles)
Car Parking: Available on site
Coach Parking: Available on site
Souvenir Shop(s): Yes
Food & Drinks: Available

SPECIAL INFORMATION

The railway is situated in Hidden Valley Discovery Park which contains a number of other attractions including a garden railway with over 1,000 feet of track and the 'Crystal Challenges' area.

OPERATING INFORMATION

Opening Times: 2013 dates: Daily from 27th May to 29th September but closed on most Saturdays, except for during August. Also open during October half-term and for much of December. Open from 10.00am to 5.00pm with the last admission at 3.00pm each day.
Steam Working: Sundays and Wednesdays.
Prices: Adult £8.95
       Child £7.95 (Free for ages 4 and under)
       Concession £7.95
       Family £30.00
Note: The above prices are for entry into the Park which includes the cost of train rides.

Detailed Directions by Car:
Take the A30 from Exeter towards Bodmin and then (shortly after Launceston) take the A395 towards Davidstow and Bude. After about one mile, turn right following the brown tourist signs for 'Hidden Valley'. The railway is located in the Discovery Park approximately ¾ mile along this road.

PORTHMADOG WOODLAND RAILWAY

Address: Tremadog Road, Porthmadog, Gwynedd LL49 9DY
Telephone Nº: (01766) 513402
Year Formed: 1961
Location of Line: At the Welsh Highland Heritage Railway
Length of Line: 550 yards

Nº of Steam Locos: 3 (at the WHR)
Nº of Other Locos: 18 (at the WHR)
Nº of Members: 1,000
Annual Membership Fee: £25.00 Adult
Approx Nº of Visitors P.A.: 25,000
Gauge: 7¼ inches
Web site: www.whr.co.uk

GENERAL INFORMATION

Nearest Mainline Station: Porthmadog (adjacent)
Nearest Bus Station: Services 1 & 3 stop 50 yards away
Car Parking: Free parking at site, plus a public Pay and Display car park within 100 yards
Coach Parking: Adjacent
Souvenir Shop(s): Yes – large range available
Food & Drinks: Yes – excellent home cooking at the Russell Team Room!

SPECIAL INFORMATION

The Porthmadog Woodland Railway is located at the Welsh Highland Heritage Railway. Tickets for the WHHR entitle customers to free rides on the Woodland Railway.

OPERATING INFORMATION

Opening Times: 2013 dates: Daily from 26th March to 3rd November inclusive (closed on some Mondays and Fridays during September & October). Trains run at 10.30am, 11.30am, 1.00pm, 2.00pm, 3.00pm and 4.00pm (the last train runs at 3.00pm during October and November).
Steam Working: 7th to 15th April; 5th to 7th May; 2nd to 4th June; Weekends in June and July then daily from 21st July to 2nd September; Weekends in September; 20th to 28th October.
Prices: Adult Day Rover £7.50
            Child Day Rover £3.75   (Under-5s free)
            Senior Citizen Day Rover £6.00
            Family Day Rover £18.50
                    (2 adults + 2 children)

Detailed Directions by Car:

From Bangor/Caernarfon take the A487 to Porthmadog. From Pwllheli take the A497 to Porthmadog then turn left at the roundabout. From the Midlands take A487 to Portmadog. Once in Porthmadog, follow the brown tourist signs. The line is located right next to Porthmadog Mainline Station, opposite the Queens Hotel.

RAINSBROOK VALLEY RAILWAY

Address: Rugby Model Engineering
Society, Onley Lane, Rugby CV22 5QD
Telephone Nº: (01788) 330238
Year Formed: 1949
Location of Line: Onley Lane, Rugby
Length of Line: 1,100 yards ground level
(7¼ inch) and also 1,100 feet elevated
(2½, 3½ & 5 inch gauges)

Nº of Steam Locos: 10
Nº of Other Locos: 4+
Nº of Members: 90
Annual Membership Fee: £45.00
Approx Nº of Visitors P.A.: 6,000
Gauges: 3½ inches, 5 inches & 7¼ inches
Web site: www.rugbymes.co.uk

GENERAL INFORMATION

Nearest Mainline Station: Rugby (2½ miles)
Nearest Bus Station: Rugby (2½ miles)
Car Parking: Available on site
Coach Parking: None
Souvenir Shop(s): None
Food & Drinks: Light refreshments only

SPECIAL INFORMATION

The Rainsbrook Valley Railway is operated by
members of the Rugby Model Engineering Society Ltd.

OPERATING INFORMATION

Opening Times: 2013 dates: 21st April, 19th May,
16th June, 20th & 21st July, 18th August, 15th
September and 20th October.
Steam Working: Trains run from 2.00pm to 5.00pm
Prices: £1.20 per ride (Under-3s travel free)

Detailed Directions by Car:
From the M1: Exit at Junction 18 and follow the A428 westwards towards Rugby. After 3 miles turn left on to the
B4429 towards Dunchurch. After 1 mile turn left at the crossroads into Onley Lane and the Railway is on the right
hand side after 300 yards; From Dunchurch: Follow the A426 Northwards then turn onto the B4429 at the
roundabout travelling Eastwards. After 1 mile turn right at the crossroads into Onley Lane for the Railway; From
Rugby: In Rugby, follow signs for the Hospital in Barby Road then continue South for 1 mile. At the crossroads
go straight on over the B4429 into Onley Lane for the Railway.

READING SOCIETY OF MODEL ENGINEERS

Address: Prospect Park, Bath Road, Reading, Berkshire RG30 2BQ
Telephone Nº: (0118) 959-9732
Year Formed: 1909 (line since 1975)
Location of Line: Prospect Park, Reading
Length of Line: Two lines, one of 1,050 feet and one of 1,300 feet

Nº of Steam Locos: Approximately 100
Nº of Other Locos: Approximately 20
Nº of Members: 130
Annual Membership Fee: £42.00
Approx Nº of Visitors P.A.: 8,000
Gauge: 2½ inches, 3½ inches, 5 inches and 7¼ inches
Web site: www.rsme.co.uk

GENERAL INFORMATION

Nearest Mainline Station: Reading (2 miles)
Nearest Bus Station: Reading Station (2 miles)
Car Parking: Available on site
Coach Parking: Available by prior arrangement
Souvenir Shop(s): None
Food & Drinks: Available

SPECIAL INFORMATION

The Reading SME has been using the current site for more than 40 years and it now boasts a well equipped club house and useful workshop facilities.

OPERATING INFORMATION

Opening Times: The first Sunday of the month throughout the year plus some Bank Holiday Sundays. Trains run from 1.00pm to 5.00pm (until 4.00pm during the Winter months).
Steam Working: All operating days
Prices: 60p per ride

Detailed Directions by Car:

Exit the M4 at Junction 12 and take the A4 Bath Road towards Reading. Continue on this road for approximately 2¼ miles. Prospect Park is on the left, continue along Bath Road almost to the end of Prospect Park and the entrance to the car park for the railway is on the left about 100 metres before the traffic lights.

ROCHDALE S.M.E.E.

Address: Springfield Park, Rochdale, OL11 4RF
Telephone Nº: None
Year Formed: 1935
Location of Line: Rochdale, Lancashire
Length of Line: 1,900 feet

Nº of Steam Locos: 1 (+ Members' locos)
Nº of Other Locos: 1
Nº of Members: Approximately 85
Annual Membership Fee: £20.00
Approx Nº of Visitors P.A.: 3,500
Gauges: 3½ inches, 5 inches & 7¼ inches
Web site: www.rsmee.com

GENERAL INFORMATION

Nearest Mainline Station: Rochdale (1 mile)
Nearest Bus Station: Rochdale (1 mile)
Car Parking: Available on site
Coach Parking: Available
Souvenir Shop(s): None
Food & Drinks: None

SPECIAL INFORMATION

The Rochdale Society of Model and Experimental Engineers welcomes visiting locomotives to their Springfield Park location. Current boiler certificates and insurance are required.

OPERATING INFORMATION

Opening Times: Sundays from April until the end of October, from 2.00pm to 4.30pm.
Steam Working: Every operating day.
Prices: 50p per ride

Detailed Directions by Car:
From All Parts: Exit the M62 at Junction 20 and take the A627(M) towards Rochdale. Continue onto the A664 then turn left onto the A58. The Park is located on the right about ½ mile along the A58 Bolton Road.

ROSEHILL VICTORIA PARK RAILWAY

Address: Victoria Park, Rawmarsh, Rotherham   S62 7JS
Telephone Nº: (01709) 703794
Year Formed: 1994
Location: Rawmarsh Victoria Park
Length of Line: 412 yards (ground level) and 178 yards (raised track)

Nº of Steam Locos: 1
Nº of Other Locos: 1
Nº of Members: Approximately 65
Annual Membership Fee: £20.00
Approx Nº of Visitors P.A.: 4,000
Gauges: 3½ inches, 5 inches & 7¼ inches
Web site: www.rdmes.co.uk

GENERAL INFORMATION

Nearest Mainline Station: Rotherham Central (4 miles)
Nearest Bus Station: Rotherham (4 miles)
Car Parking: Available on site
Coach Parking: Not available
Souvenir Shop(s): None
Food & Drinks: None

SPECIAL INFORMATION

The Rosehill Victoria Park Railway is operated by members of the Rotherham & District Model Engineers Society.

OPERATING INFORMATION

Opening Times: Sundays from Easter until the end of October and also Wednesdays during the School Holidays. Trains run from 12.30pm to 4.30pm.
Steam Working: Occasional Sundays only. Please contact the Society or check their web site for further information.
Prices: 50p per ride

Detailed Directions by Car:
From All Parts: Exit the M1 at Junction 33 and take the A630 (Centenary Way) to the A633, signposted for Parkgate Retail Park. Pass the retail park, continue on A633 for 1½ miles, pass the Stagecoach Bus Station and, after about 100 yards, turn left into Rosehill Road after the petrol station. At the end of Rosehill Road, turn right into Birchwood Avenue then take the first right into Park Grove for access to the Park along a public track.

ROXBOURNE PARK MINIATURE RAILWAY

Address: Roxbourne Park, Field End Road, Eastcote, Middlesex	**Nº of Steam Locos**: Members locos only
Telephone Nº: None	**Nº of Other Locos**: Members locos only
Year Formed: 1936	**Nº of Members**: Approximately 128
Location of Line: Roxbourne Park	**Approx Nº of Visitors P.A.**: 2,500
Length of Line: 2,200 feet	**Gauge**: 3½ inches, 5 inches & 7¼ inches
	Web site: www.hwsme.org

GENERAL INFORMATION

Nearest Tube Station: Eastcote (½ mile)
Nearest Bus Station: –
Car Parking: Free parking is available on site
Coach Parking: None
Food & Drinks: None

SPECIAL INFORMATION

The railway is operated by members of the Harrow & Wembley Society of Model Engineers which has been running passenger services on the current track in Roxbourne Park since 1979.

OPERATING INFORMATION

Opening Times: 2013 dates: Every Sunday from 31st March to 20th October inclusive with a special Halloween run on 27th October. Trains run from 2.30pm to 5.00pm. Santa trains also operate on 15th December from 1.00pm to 4.00pm.
For details of further special events, please check the society's web site.
Steam Working: Every operating day.
Prices: £1.00 per ride

Detailed Directions by Car:
Exit the M40 at Target roundabout and travel into Northolt Village on the A312. Turn left into Eastcote Lane North after the traffic lights just after Northolt Station and continue along this road. Eastcote Lane becomes Field End Road and Roxbourne Park is a little further on opposite Venue '5' (formerly The Clay Pigeon Public House).

RYEDALE SOCIETY OF MODEL ENGINEERS

Address: The Old School, Pottergate, Gilling East, North Yorkshire   YO62 4JJ
Telephone Nº: None
Year Formed: 1983
Location of Line: Gilling East
Length of Line: 450 metres

Nº of Steam Locos: 10
Nº of Other Locos: Several
Nº of Members: 60
Annual Membership Fee: £50.00
Approx Nº of Visitors P.A.: 3,500
Gauge: 3½ inches, 5 inches and 7¼ inches
Web site: www.rsme.org.uk

GENERAL INFORMATION

Nearest Mainline Station: Thirsk (11 miles)
Nearest Bus Station: Helmsley (5 miles)
Car Parking: Available on site
Coach Parking: Available
Souvenir Shop(s): None
Food & Drinks: Available

OPERATING INFORMATION

Opening Times: 2013 dates: Easter Sunday then every Sunday to 29th September except for 28th April, 19th May and 25th August which are special event days for spectators only (no rides available). Open from 12.30pm to 4.30pm.
Steam Working: Every operating day.
Prices: 75p per ride

Detailed Directions by Car:
Gilling East is situated approximately 3 miles south of Helmsley (which is on the A170 Thirsk to Scarborough road). Gilling East is on the B1363 which joins the B1257 at nearby Oswaldkirk. Head West at the crossroads by the Fairfax Arms, signposted for the Golf Club and The Old School is situated on the right after around 200 yards.

Saffron Walden & District s.m.e.

Correspondence: Derek Wheddon,
67 Crescent Road, Heybridge, Maldon,
Essex CM9 4SN
Telephone Nº: (01621) 858634
Year Formed: 1980
Location: Audley End Miniature Railway
Length of Line: 1,300 feet

Nº of Steam Locos: 14
Nº of Other Locos: 8
Nº of Members: 60
Approx Nº of Visitors P.A.: 4,000
Gauge: 3½ inches, 5 inches & 7¼ inches
Web site: www.swdsme.org.uk
E-mail: derek@dwheddon.freeserve.co.uk

GENERAL INFORMATION

Nearest Mainline Station: Audley End (1 mile)
Nearest Bus Station: Saffron Walden (1 mile)
Car Parking: Available on site
Coach Parking: Available on site
Souvenir Shop(s): Yes
Food & Drinks: Snacks available

SPECIAL INFORMATION

The Saffron Walden & District Society of Model
Engineers uses a track at Audley End Steam Railway,
Lord Braybrooke's 10¼ inch railway situated just
next to Audley End House, an English Heritage site.

OPERATING INFORMATION

Opening Times: On Saturdays and Sundays from
Easter to the end of October, Club members are
usually on hand to give rides on our railway using
steam, electric or diesel locomotives. There is also a
very attractive picnic/play area next to the station.
The railway is also open during some additional
weekdays in the school holidays. Check the club's
website for additional dates and events or contact
the club directly. Rides are usually available from
around Noon on operating days.
Steam Working: Most operating days.
Prices: £1.00 per ride (A Multi-ride ticket is £3.00)

Detailed Directions by Car:
Exit the M11 at Junction 10 if southbound or Junction 9 if northbound and follow the signs for Audley End
House. The railway is situated just across the road from Audley End House.

SAUSMAREZ MANOR MINIATURE RAILWAY

Address: Sausmarez Road, St. Martins, Guernsey, Channel Islands GY4 6SG **Telephone Nº**: (01481) 235571 **Year Formed**: 1985 **Location of Line**: Guernsey **Length of Line**: 400 yards	**Nº of Steam Locos**: None **Nº of Other Locos**: 2 **Nº of Members**: – **Approx Nº of Visitors P.A.**: 4,000 **Gauge**: 7¼ inches **Web site**: www.sausmarezmanor.co.uk

Remus and friends at Sausmarez Manor.

GENERAL INFORMATION

Nearest Mainline Station: Not applicable
Nearest Bus Station: Not applicable
Car Parking: Available on site
Coach Parking: Available
Souvenir Shop(s): Yes
Food & Drinks: Available

SPECIAL INFORMATION

The railway runs through the grounds of Sausmarez Manor, a stately home which dates back to the 13th Century.

OPERATING INFORMATION

Opening Times: Weekends from May to September and also daily during the School Holidays. Trains run from 10.00am to 4.00pm.
Steam Working: None
Prices: Adults £2.00
Children £1.50
Concessions £1.50
Family Tickets £5.00

Detailed Directions by Car:
Sausmarez Manor is situated 1½ mile to the south of St. Peter's Port, Guernsey.

SCOTTISH MODEL ENGINEERING TRUST

Address: Wester Pickston Railway, College Road, Glenalmond PH1 3RX
Telephone Nº: (01764) 653660
Year Formed: 2003
Location: Glenalmond, near Perth
Length of Line: ¾ mile

Nº of Steam Locos: Members' locos only
Nº of Other Locos: Members' locos only
Nº of Members: Approximately 65
Annual Membership Fee: See web site
Approx Nº of Visitors P.A.: 7,500
Gauges: 3½ inches, 5 inches & 7¼ inches
Web site: www.smet.org.uk

GENERAL INFORMATION

Nearest Mainline Station: Perth (10 miles)
Nearest Bus Station: Perth (10 miles)
Car Parking: Available on site
Coach Parking: Available
Souvenir Shop(s): Yes
Food & Drinks: Available

SPECIAL INFORMATION

The Trust was formed in 2001 with the aim of demonstrating Scotland's engineering heritage through exhibitions, lectures and the sharing of the hobby in general.

OPERATING INFORMATION

Opening Times: 2013 dates: 14th April, 19th May, 4th August and 1st September.
Open from 11.30am to 4.00pm on these days.
Steam Working: All open days.
Prices: £1.50 per ride or 4 rides for £5.00

Detailed Directions by Car:
From All Parts: Take the A85 from Perth to Methven and turn right onto College Road opposite the Post Office. The railway is 3 miles to the north of Methven on the right-hand side of the road.

Spenborough M. & E.E. ltd

| **Contact Address**: Mike Duncan, 11 Heather Court, Birstall, Batley, WF17 9BD
Telephone Nº: (01924) 474164
Year Formed: 1950
Location: Royds Park, Spenborough, BD19 5LL | **Length of Line**: One tenth of a mile
Nº of Steam Locos: 3 (+ members locos)
Nº of Other Locos: 2 (+ members locos)
Nº of Members: 24
Approx Nº of Visitors P.A.: 3,000
Gauge: 3½ inches, 5 inches & 7¼ inches
Web site: www.spenborough.me.uk |

GENERAL INFORMATION

Nearest Mainline Station: Dewsbury (5 miles)
Nearest Bus Station: Cleckheaton
Car Parking: Approximately 20 spaces on site
Coach Parking: None
Food & Drinks: Light refreshments available

SPECIAL INFORMATION

Spenborough Model & Experimental Engineers operate their service on two tracks in Royds Park which are built on the trackbed of the old London & North West Railway. The club operates a Cromar white carriage for wheelchair passengers.

OPERATING INFORMATION

Opening Times: 2013 dates: 31st March; 14th & 28th April; 5th & 26th May; 9th & 23rd June; 14th, 24th, 28th & 31st July; 7th, 11th, 14th, 21st, 25th & 28th August; 8th & 22nd September; 13th & 27th October; 3rd November and 15th December. Trains run from 1.00pm to 4.30pm.
Steam Working: Most operating days.
Prices: £1.00 per ride (3 circuits of the track).

Detailed Directions by Car:
Exit the M62 at Junction 26 and turn off at the roundabout onto the A638 Cleckheaton to Dewsbury road. Travel through Cleckheaton for approximately ¾ mile then, just after the start of the dual carriageway, turn left onto New Street and at the top of the street is the entrance to Royds Park.

STANSTED PARK LIGHT RAILWAY

Address: Stansted House, Rowlands Castle PO9 6DX **Telephone Nº**: (023) 9241-3324 **Year Formed**: 2005 **Location**: Rowlands Castle, Hampshire **Length of Line**: ½ mile	**Nº of Steam Locos**: 5 **Nº of Other Locos**: 3 **Approx Nº of Visitors P.A.**: 20,000 **Gauge**: 7¼ inches **Web site**: www.splr.info

GENERAL INFORMATION

Nearest Mainline Station: Rowlands Castle (1¼ miles)
Nearest Bus Station: Hilsea Portsmouth (5 miles)
Car Parking: Available on site
Coach Parking: Available
Souvenir Shop(s): At the Garden Centre
Food & Drinks: Available

SPECIAL INFORMATION

The railway is located within the grounds of Stansted House which stands in 1,800 acres of ancient forest on the South Downs.

OPERATING INFORMATION

Opening Times: Wednesdays, weekends and Bank Holidays throughout the year and daily during the School Holidays. Trains run from 10.00am to 4.00pm.
Steam Working: Most opening days during the Summer, weather permitting.
Prices: Adults £2.00
Children £1.50 (Free for Under-2s)
Concessions £1.50

Detailed Directions by Car:
From All Parts: Exit the A3(M) at Junction 2 and take the B2149 towards Rowlands Castle.

STRATHAVEN MINIATURE RAILWAY

Address: George Allan Park, Threestanes Road, Strathaven   ML10 6EF
Telephone Nº: (0141) 641-5478
Year Formed: 1974
Location of Line: George Allan Park
Length of Line: 1,425 feet

Nº of Steam Locos: 3 (+ Members locos)
Nº of Other Locos: 2
Nº of Members: Approximately 30
Approx Nº of Visitors P.A.: 8,500
Gauges: 3¼ inches, 5 inches & 7¼ inches
Website: None

GENERAL INFORMATION

Nearest Mainline Station: Hamilton (8 miles)
Nearest Bus Station: Hamilton (8 miles)
Car Parking: Available on site
Coach Parking: Available
Souvenir Shop(s): None
Food & Drinks: Available in the Park

SPECIAL INFORMATION

The railway is operated by members of the Strathaven Model Society.

OPERATING INFORMATION

Opening Times: Weekends and Bank Holiday Mondays from Easter until the end of September. Trains run from 1.00pm to 4.30pm.
Steam Working: Most operating days, weather permitting.
Prices: £1.00 per ride

Detailed Directions by Car:
From All Parts: Exit the M74 at Junction 8 and take the A71 through Stonehouse to Strathaven. Turn right onto the A726 and George Allan Park is on the left hand side of the road.

STRAWBERRY LINE MINIATURE RAILWAY

Address: Avon Valley Country Park, Pixash Lane, Keynsham, Bristol, BS31 1TF
Telephone Nº: (0117) 986-0124
Year Formed: 1999
Location: Avon Valley Country Park
Length of Line: Two-thirds of a mile

Nº of Steam Locos: 4
Nº of Other Locos: 20
Approx Nº of Visitors P.A.: 100,000
Gauge: 5 inches
Web site: www.strawberryminirail.co.uk

GENERAL INFORMATION

Nearest Mainline Station: Keynsham (2 miles)
Nearest Bus Station: Bath (6 miles)
Car Parking: Available on site
Coach Parking: Available
Souvenir Shop(s): Yes
Food & Drinks: Available

SPECIAL INFORMATION

The Strawberry Line operates within the Avon Valley Country Park and is the only commercial railway in the UK which uses a 5 inch gauge.

OPERATING INFORMATION

Opening Times: 2013 dates: Daily from Easter until 3rd November from 10.00am to 5.30pm.
Steam Working: Frequently – please contact the railway for further details.
Prices: £1.50 per ride
Note: There is a separate admission charge for entry into the Avon Valley Country Park:
  Adults £8.00
  Children £7.50 (Under-2s admitted free)
  Senior Citizens £7.50

Detailed Directions by Car:
From All Parts: Take the A4 from Bath or Bristol to Keynsham and turn into Pixash Lane following the brown tourist signs for the railway.

SUMMERFIELDS MINIATURE RAILWAY

Address: Rook Tree Farm, Cotton End, Bedford MK45 3BH	**Nº of Steam Locos**: 8
Telephone Nº: (01234) 743062	**Nº of Other Locos**: 7
Year Formed: 1948	**Nº of Members**: Approximately 180
Location: Off the A600, North of Haynes	**Annual Membership Fee**: £32.00
Length of Line: Approximately ¾ mile	**Approx Nº of Visitors P.A.**: 10,000
	Gauge: 3½ inches, 5 inches & 7¼ inches
	Web site: www.bedfordmes.co.uk

GENERAL INFORMATION

Nearest Mainline Station: Bedford (5½ miles)
Nearest Bus Station: Bedford
Car Parking: Available on site
Coach Parking: Available on site
Souvenir Shop(s): None
Food & Drinks: Available

SPECIAL INFORMATION

Summerfields Miniature Railways is operated by the Bedford Model Engineering Society.

OPERATING INFORMATION

Opening Times: 2013 dates: 28th April; 5th, 6th, 26th & 27th May; 23rd June; 28th July; 7th, 14th, 25th & 26th August; 22nd September and 27th October. Santa Specials run on 7th & 8th December. Trains run from 11.00am to 4.00pm.
Steam Working: On all public running days
Prices: Adult Return £1.50
Child Return £1.50

Detailed Directions by Car:
From All Parts: The Railway is located by the A600 just to the North of Haynes, 5½ miles South of Bedford and 3½ miles North of Shefford.

SURREY SOCIETY OF MODEL ENGINEERS

Address: Mill Lane, Leatherhead, Surrey, KT22 9AA (No post please as the site does not have a letterbox!)
Telephone Nº: None
Year Formed: 1978
Location of Line: Mill Lane, Leatherhead
Length of Line: 2,000 feet

Nº of Steam Locos: 10
Nº of Other Locos: 8
Nº of Members: 48
Approx Nº of Visitors P.A.: 10,000
Gauge: Both ground and raised level tracks are available covering many gauges
Web site: www.ssme.co.uk

GENERAL INFORMATION

Nearest Mainline Station: Leatherhead (½ mile)
Nearest Bus Station: Leatherhead (½ mile)
Car Parking: Parking on a grass area is possible when conditions allow
Coach Parking: None
Food & Drinks: Available

OPERATING INFORMATION

Opening Times: Various Bank Holidays on other dates throughout the year. 2013 dates: 14th April; 6th & 27th May; 30th June; 14th July; 26th August; 8th September; 13th October.
Trains run from 11.00am to 4.00pm. Please contact the railway or check their web site for further details.
Steam Working: All operating days.
Prices: £1.00 per ride
£5.00 multi-ride ticket allows 6 rides

Detailed Directions by Car:
The railway is situated near Leatherhead town centre. Mill Lane is across the road from the well signposted Leisure Centre just off the B2122 Waterway Road and just a short walk to the south of Leatherhead Mainline station.

SWANLEY NEW BARN RAILWAY

Address: Swanley Park, New Barn Road, Swanley   BR8 7PW
Telephone Nº: None
Year Formed: 1986
Location of Line: Swanley, Kent
Length of Line: 900 yards

Nº of Steam Locos: 8
Nº of Other Locos: 10
Approx Nº of Visitors P.A.: Not known
Gauge: 7¼ inches
Web site: www.snbr.20m.com

GENERAL INFORMATION

Nearest Mainline Station: Swanley (¾ mile)
Nearest Bus Station: Swanley (¾ mile)
Car Parking: Available on site
Coach Parking: Available
Souvenir Shop(s): None
Food & Drinks: Available in the Park

SPECIAL INFORMATION

The railway is located in a Swanley Park which also has play areas, paddling pool, sandpit, boating lake, cafeteria, bouncy castle and battery bikes all set in 60 acres of parkland with free access and parking.

OPERATING INFORMATION

Opening Times: 2013 dates: Weekends and most days during the School Holidays from Easter to 3rd November. Trains run from 11.00am to 5.00pm.
Steam Working: Regular steam working but on an ad hoc basis.
Prices: Adult Return £1.50
              Child Return £1.00
              Family Return £4.00 (2 adults + 2 children)

Detailed Directions by Car:
From All Parts: Exit the M25 at Junction 3 and follow green signs for Swanley Park. Go straight on at the first roundabout then turn right at the second roundabout. Continue straight on at the next roundabout then turn left at the next crossroads into New Barn Road. The Park is on the left side of the road.

THAMES DITTON MINIATURE RAILWAY

Address: Willowbank, Claygate Lane, Thames Ditton, Surrey KT7 0LE
Telephone Nº: (020) 8398 3985
Year Formed: 1936
Location of Line: Thames Ditton
Length of Line: ½ mile

Nº of Steam Locos: 30+
Nº of Other Locos: 10+
Nº of Members: Approximately 200
Approx Nº of Visitors P.A.: 15,000
Gauge: 3½ inches, 5 inches & 7¼ inches
Web site: www.malden-dsme.co.uk

GENERAL INFORMATION

Nearest Mainline Station: Thames Ditton (½ mile)
Nearest Bus Station: Thames Ditton
Car Parking: Street parking only
Coach Parking: None
Souvenir Shop(s): Yes
Food & Drinks: Available from 2.30pm onwards

SPECIAL INFORMATION

The railway is operated by Malden and District Society of Model Engineers, is well known locally and is referred to as the Thames Ditton Miniature Railway. The Society operates two tracks at the site – a ground level railway is for larger trains and an elevated railway is for the smaller scale trains. Both are used for passenger hauling services.

OPERATING INFORMATION

Opening Times: Open on Easter Sunday and Monday then the first Sunday of each month and every Bank Holiday Sunday and Monday until the first Sunday in October. Trains run from 2.00pm to 5.30pm though the site is open from 1.00pm onwards. Also open during dates in December for pre-booked Santa Specials – please check the web site for further details.
Steam Working: Every operating day.
Prices: Single ride tickets £2.50
  Unlimited ride tickets £6.50
  Family tickets £23.00

Detailed Directions by Car:
Claygate Lane is located just off the A307 Esher to Kingston road about half a mile to the East of the junction between the A307 and A309. If travelling from the East, Claygate Lane is the turning on the left immediately before the railway bridge. If travelling from the West, Claygate Lane is immediately after the second railway bridge though there is unfortunately, no right turn allowed from this direction.

TONBRIDGE MODEL ENGINEERING SOCIETY

Address: The Slade, Castle Grounds, Tonbridge, Kent TN9 1HR
Telephone Nº: (01892) 538415
Year Formed: 1944
Location: Castle Grounds, Tonbridge
Length of Line: ¼ mile

Nº of Steam Locos: 40
Nº of Other Locos: 1
Nº of Members: Approximately 100
Approx Nº of Visitors P.A.: 14,000
Gauge: 3½ inches and 5 inches
Web site: www.tmes.pwp.blueyonder.co.uk

GENERAL INFORMATION

Nearest Mainline Station: Tonbridge (1 mile)
Nearest Bus Station: Tonbridge (1 mile)
Car Parking: Available on site
Coach Parking: None
Food & Drinks: Available

SPECIAL INFORMATION

The Society has run a track at the present site since 1951 and since then facilities have been extended to include a steaming bay and turntable, passenger trollies, refreshment facilities and meeting room, store, and a well appointed workshop.

OPERATING INFORMATION

Opening Times: 2013 dates: Saturday and Sunday afternoons from 24th March to the end of September, weather permitting. Please contact the railway for further information.
Steam Working: Every operating day.
Prices: Free of charge but donations are accepted.

Detailed Directions by Car:
Exit the A21 Tonbridge Bypass at the junction signposted for Tonbridge South. Drive up the High Street, cross over the River Medway and turn left by the sign for the Swimming Pool. Follow the road round, turn left at Slade School and the car park for the railway is directly ahead.

VOGRIE PARK MINIATURE RAILWAY

Contact Address: Eskvalley MES,
Roslin Glen Country Park, Roslin,
Midlothian   EH25 9PX
Phone Nº: (01875) 856687 (President)
Year Formed: 1982
Location of Line: Vogrie Country Park
Length of Line: 2000 feet

Nº of Steam Locos: 5 (Member's locos)
Nº of Other Locos: 5
Nº of Members: 30
Approx Nº of Visitors P.A.: 6,000
Gauge: 5 inches and 7¼ inches
Web site: www.eskvalleymes.org.uk
E-mail: vpmr@btinternet.com

GENERAL INFORMATION

Nearest Mainline Station: Edinburgh (9 miles)
Nearest Bus Station: Dalkeith (3 miles)
Car Parking: Available on site
Coach Parking: Available on site
Food & Drinks: Available on site

SPECIAL INFORMATION

The Eskvalley MES operates a railway in the grounds
of the Vogrie Country Park which comprises 105
hectares of woods and Victorian parkland including
a 1876 Victorian mansion (part of which is open to
the public), a nine-hole golf course, adventure
playground and a cafeteria.

OPERATING INFORMATION

Opening Times: Sundays from Easter to September.
Trains run from 2.00pm to 5.00pm.
Steam Working: Most operating days.
Prices: £1.00 per person per ride.
Party bookings can be arranged on other days.
Please phone Geoff on (01875) 823388 or Robin on
07959 856687 for further information.

Detailed Directions by Car:
From Dalkeith: Travel South on the A68 for 2½ miles then turn right onto the B6372 signposted for Vogrie
Country Park. Continue along this road for the Park; From the A7: Travel towards Gorbridge and turn off onto
the B6372. Pass through Gorbridge staying on the B6372, continue through Newlandrig for the Park.

WELLINGTON COUNTRY PARK RAILWAY

Address: Odiham Road, Riseley, RG7 1SP
Telephone Nº: (0118) 932-6444
Year Formed: 1980
Location of Line: Riseley, Berkshire
Length of Line: 500 yards

Nº of Steam Locos: None
Nº of Other Locos: 1
Nº of Members: –
Approx Nº of Visitors P.A.: Not known
Gauge: 7¼ inches
Web site: www.wellington-country-park.co.uk

GENERAL INFO

Nearest Mainline Station:
Mortimer (5 miles)
Nearest Bus Station:
Reading (9 miles)
Car Parking: Available on site
Coach Parking: Available
Souvenir Shop(s): Yes
Food & Drinks: Available

SPECIAL INFORMATION

The railway is located within 350 acres of beautiful parklands which surround a 35 acre lake.

OPERATING INFO

Opening Times:
2013 dates: Daily from 16th February until 3rd November. Open from 9.30am to 5.00pm (but until 4.00pm during the Winter).
Steam Working: None
Prices:
Adults £9.00 (Park Admission)
Children £8.00 (Park Admission)
Under-3s are admitted free
Senior Citizens £8.50
  (Park Admission)
Family Tickets £31.50
  (2 adults + 2 children)
Note: Train rides are an additional £1.50 each.

Detailed Directions by Car:
From All Parts: Exit the M4 at Junction 11 and take the A33 towards Basingstoke. Turn onto the B3349 at the Riseley roundabout and follow the signs to the Park which is straight off the roundabout.

WESTON PARK RAILWAY

Address: Weston Park, Weston-under-Lizard, Shifnal, Shropshire TF11 8LE
Telephone Nº: (05601) 132334 (Railway) or (01952) 852100 (Weston Park)
Year Formed: 1980
Location of Line: Weston Park
Length of Line: Approximately 1¼ miles

Nº of Steam Locos: Variable
Nº of Other Locos: Variable
Approx Nº of Visitors P.A.: 19,500
Gauge: 7¼ inches
Web site: www.westonrail.co.uk
E-mail: bruce@westonrail.co.uk

GENERAL INFORMATION

Nearest Mainline Station: Shifnal (6 miles)
Nearest Bus Station: –
Car Parking: Available on site
Coach Parking: Available on site
Souvenir Shop(s): –
Food & Drinks: Available

SPECIAL INFORMATION

The railway operates in the grounds of Weston Park (www.weston-park.com), a stately home with a large park and gardens designed by 'Capability' Brown. Weston Park also has a number of other attractions for all the family.

OPERATING INFORMATION

Opening Times: 2013 dates: 30th March to 14th April then daily from 25th May to 8th September. Please note that the railway closes during the V Festival which is from 14th to 21st August 2013.
Steam Working: Please contact the railway for further details: info@westonrail.co.uk
Prices: Adults £2.00
Children £2.00
Note: Prices shown above are for train fares only. An admission charge is made for entry into the park, gardens and stately home. This admission fee is required for use of the railway. Please contact Weston Park for admission price information:
West Park Web site: www.weston-park.com

Detailed Directions by Car:
From All Parts: Weston Park is situated by the side of the A5 in Weston-under-Lizard, Shropshire, just 3 miles from the M54 (exit at Junction 3 and take the A41 northwards) and 8 miles West of the M6 (exit at Junction 12).

WEST RIDING SMALL LOCOMOTIVE SOCIETY

Address: The rear of Freedom House, Bradford Road, Tingley, Wakefield, WF3 1SD	**N° of Steam Locos**: Numerous
	N° of Other Locos: Numerous
	N° of Members: 85
Telephone N°: (01924) 363908	**Annual Membership Fee**: £25.00
Year Formed: 1945	**Approx N° of Visitors P.A.**: 1,200
Location of Line: Tingley, Wakefield	**Gauge**: A number of gauges including:
Length of Line: 650 feet	7¼", 5", 3½" and 2½ inches
Web site: www.westridingsmalllocomotivessociety.20m.com	

GENERAL INFORMATION

Nearest Mainline Station: Wakefield (4 miles)
Nearest Bus Station: Wakefield (4 miles)
Car Parking: Available on site
Coach Parking: Available
Souvenir Shop(s): None
Food & Drinks: Available in the Clubhouse

OPERATING INFORMATION

Opening Times: Every Sunday from Easter to October. Open from 1.30pm to 4.30pm.
Steam Working: Every operating day.
Prices: 50p per ride (or £1.80 for 4 rides)

Detailed Directions by Car:
Exit the M62 at Junction 28 and take the A650 towards Wakefield. Turn left just after the 2nd set of traffic lights for Freedom House. The track is located at the rear of Freedom House. Alternatively, exit the M1 at Junction 41 and take the A650 towards Bradford. Freedom House is ½ mile past the traffic lights on the right.

WILLEN LAKE MINIATURE RAILWAY

Address: South Willen Lake,
Milton Keynes   MK15 0DS
Telephone Nº: 07810 131737
Year Formed: 1989
Location of Line: Milton Keynes
Length of Line: 600 yards

Nº of Steam Locos: None
Nº of Other Locos: 1
Approx Nº of Visitors P.A.: More than
one million visitors to the Park each year
Gauge: 7¼ inches
Web site: www.whitecap.co.uk

GENERAL INFORMATION

Nearest Mainline Station: Milton Keynes Central
(1½ miles)
Nearest Bus Station: Milton Keynes (1½ miles)
Car Parking: Available on site
Coach Parking: Available
Souvenir Shop(s): None
Food & Drinks: Available

OPERATING INFORMATION

Opening Times: Weekends and daily during the
School Holidays from April until the end of
October. Open from 11.00am to 5.00pm.
Steam Working: None
Prices: £1.50 per ride

Detailed Directions by Car:
From All Parts: Exit the M1 at Junction 14 and follow the H6 towards Milton Keynes. The lake is to the left of the
road by the V10 (Brickhill Street).

WOKING MINIATURE RAILWAY

Address: Barrs Lane, Knaphill, Woking, Surrey   GU21 2JW
Telephone Nº: (01483) 720801
E-mail: mizensrailway@btinternet.com
Year Formed: 1989
Location of Line: Knaphill, Surrey
Length of Line: 1 mile

Nº of Steam Locos: 10
Nº of Other Locos: 6
Nº of Members: 120
Annual Membership Fee: £15.00
Approx Nº of Visitors P.A.: 20,000
Gauge: 7¼ inches
Web site: www.mizensrailway.co.uk

GENERAL INFORMATION

Nearest Mainline Station: Woking
Nearest Bus Station: Woking
Car Parking: 200 spaces available on site
Coach Parking: Available on site
Souvenir Shop(s): Yes
Food & Drinks: Available on running days

SPECIAL INFORMATION

The Railway is situated in a beautiful location amidst 8 acres of woodland. In addition to over a mile of track, the railway has three stations, two signalboxes, a tunnel, a Roundhouse Engine Shed, a level crossing and authentic buildings.

OPERATING INFORMATION

Opening Times: Easter Sunday then every Sunday from May to September. Also Thursdays in August. Trains run from 2.00pm to 5.00pm. See the web site for details of Special Events including Santa Specials in December when pre-booking is essential.
Steam Working: Most operating days
Prices: Adult Return From £2.00
　　　　　 Child Return From £2.00
Note: Prices vary depending on the route.

Detailed Directions by Car:
From All Parts: Exit the M25 at Junction 11 and follow the A320 to Woking. At the Six Cross Roads Roundabout take the 5th exit towards Knaphill then turn left at the roundabout onto Littlewick Road. Continue along Littlewick Road crossing the roundabout before turning right into Barrs Lane just before Knaphill.

WOLVERHAMPTON & DISTRICT M.E.S.

Address: Baggeridge Country Park, Near Sedgley, Staffordshire **Telephone Nº**: (01902) 753795 **Year Formed**: 1986 **Location**: Baggeridge Country Park **Length of Line**: The ground level line is 1,400 feet and the raised track is 420 feet	**Nº of Steam Locos**: 15 **Nº of Other Locos**: 7 **Nº of Members**: 60 **Approx Nº of Visitors P.A.**: Not known **Gauge**: 3½ inches, 5 inches & 7¼ inches **Website**: www.wolverhampton-dmes.co.uk

GENERAL INFORMATION

Nearest Mainline Station: Wolverhampton (7 miles)
Nearest Bus Station: Sedgley (2 miles)
Car Parking: Available on site
Coach Parking: Available on site
Food & Drinks: Available

SPECIAL INFORMATION

The Wolverhampton & District Model Engineering Society operates the railway which runs through the Baggeridge Country Park. This was formerly the Baggeridge Colliery and part of the original Himley Estate of the Earls of Dudley. Since the closure of the Colliery, the site has been transformed into 150 acres of attractive country park.

OPERATING INFORMATION

Opening Times: 2013 dates: 1st & 21st April; 5th, 6th, 20th, 26th & 27th May; 1st, 2nd, 9th & 23rd June; 7th, 20th, 21st & 28th July; 4th, 11th, 18th, 25th & 26th August; 1st, 15th & 29th September. Trains run from 1.00pm to 5.00pm, weather permitting.
Steam Working: Most operating days.
Prices: No charge but donations are accepted.

Detailed Directions by Car:
Take the A449 Wolverhampton to Kidderminster road then turn onto the A463 towards Sedgley. Baggeridge Country Park is just to the South of the A463 after approximately 2 miles and it is well-signposted from the road.

WOODSEAVES RAILWAY

Address: Woodseaves Garden Plants, Sydnall Lane Nursery, Woodseaves, Market Drayton   TF9 2AS
Telephone Nº: (01630) 653161
Year Formed: 2004
Location of Line: Shropshire
Length of Line: Over 400 yards

Nº of Steam Locos: 1
Nº of Other Locos: 1
Approx Nº of Visitors P.A.: 1,200
Gauge: 7¼ inches
Web site: www.woodseavesminirail.co.uk

GENERAL INFORMATION

Nearest Mainline Station: Shrewsbury (19 miles)
Nearest Bus Station: Market Drayton (3 miles)
Car Parking: Available on site
Coach Parking: A small amount of space available
Souvenir Shop(s): None
Food & Drinks: Available in the Tea Shed

SPECIAL INFORMATION

The railway is constantly evolving with extensions to the track and additions to stock and infrastructure.

OPERATING INFORMATION

Opening Times: Sundays from Spring to early Autumn, 10.30am to 4.30pm. Also on some Saturdays and Bank Holidays. Please contact the railway for further details.
Steam Working: Most operating days
Prices: £1.00 per ride (Under-5s ride for free)

Detailed Directions by Car:
From All Parts: The railway is located just off the A529 at Woodseaves which is situated approximately 2 miles south of Market Drayton.
